Random Thoughts
from the
Cosmos

by
Klint of Denmark

This book is dedicated to the:

>   *Socially Unaccepted*

>   *Unloved*

>   *Unwanted*

>   *Handicapped — mentallly or physically*

>   *Unappreciated*

>   *And to those who are losers or who think they are.*

And to my wife who has been the most tolerant, understanding, and forgiving soul who ever lived. She gave me the freedom to probe and discover my other selves which had been lying dormant the first thirty years of my life.

Preface

You will discover that throughout this book there are three or four recurring themes and a great number of repetitious statements. This is by design and not by accident. If you want to say something worthwhile it bears repeating time and time again just in case the writer failed to make a lasting impression the first time. Sometimes the same concept written from a slightly different point of view or with different words will give you still another perspective.

Preface

This book is not for super-straight people

or

for those who have fixed opinions and beliefs about:

life
politics
religion
philosophy
morality
or
sex

Warning: If you have fixed opinions and beliefs this book may be hazardous to your mental health and stability.

This is a generic Bible. It is a Bible that is designed to meet the needs of people of all races, creeds, and colors. There is a lot of useful philosophy which should appeal to you whether you're an atheist, agnostic, pagan, or Christian. It is also a test to see how logical you've been in the acceptance of certain beliefs and opinions.

It covers a wide range of topics:
- *Economics • Politics • Psychology*
- *Government • Religion • Morality*
- *Philosophy • Family Values • Crime*
- *Discipline and Punishment • Justice*

It is a book on reality with no frills — stripped of all its veneer and gloss. It is a Bible that tells no stories and makes no promises. Most of what you revere as truth will be subjected to close scrutiny using "logic" as the medium for analysis.

Preface

Not all statements in this book are necessarily the author's beliefs or opinions.

Some are humorous

Some are serious

Some are controversial

Some are absurd

Many are satirical
or cynical

Most are thought provoking

A few are tongue-in-cheek

Preface

If your eye is offended by anything you read here, you may black out the quote you don't like with a black marking pen or you could get some large gummed labels and cover the quotes you find offensive. Thus, you will be able to edit the book to suit your own sense of propriety.

Please have the courage to read the entire book, but don't give up on it merely because you disagree with some of the author's philosophy. Possibly it is human nature to reject an entire book because you find one or two concepts, opinions, beliefs, or theories contrary to your own. Accept only that which resonates to your philosophy and personality and forget those you find repugnant.

Preface

This book is a liberal's answer to Rush Limbaugh. Never in the history of this country has anyone been able to mesmerize the American people like Rush Limbaugh. No one has been able to captivate audiences with his boyish charm, quick wit, and his sizzling sarcasm like Rush. No one has ever had a greater political influence on the masses since Adolph Hitler. He like Hitler preaches hate. He is a racist, anti-feminism, anti-abortion, anti-welfare and anti-homosexuality. While he is prone to ridicule everything in our culture, he seldom offers any solutions to the complex problems facing Americans today. His technique, however, is not any different than those used by the tele-evangelists and dictators. They all preach fear, guilt, and hate and are master motivators who prey upon those who seek ready answers and easy solutions.

Random Thoughts from the Cosmos

Throughout this book you will see a number of references made to tobacco usage. This book is a book on logic, psychology, sociology, as well as philosophy, but tobacco usage is the most convenient topic to study of all the substance abuses since it has been so widely publicized. Never in the history of this nation has so much hysteria been generated over a single commodity other than, perhaps, drugs — not even firearms, automobile emissions, alcohol, or food. Statistics on tobacco have been frequently quoted in the media. The question is not only what agency, organization, or government is responsible for this propaganda but who authorized the issuance of such statistics? Numbers are meaningless, but what is of greater importance is the percentage of people who die each year which can be attributed directly to

Random Thoughts from the Cosmos

*tobacco and what percentages can be
attributed to each of the other causes? Is
a smoker's life span longer or shorter
than those who do not smoke? What is
the name of the individual who assumes
responsibility for these statistics, and
what is his official capacity? What are
the mechanics and procedures for
collecting this statistical data? And can
those statistics be verified by any other
source? Could there be any political
and/or religious motives behind the
dissemination of such information?*

Random Thoughts from the Cosmos

One third of all physical illnesses are related directly or indirectly to: peer pressure, job stress, societal demands, anxiety over the future, frustration (inability to achieve goals), hopelessness, job security, parental expectations, legal restraints placed on individual freedoms, competition, economic and political trends, parental responsibilities, diet, one's appearance, racial tensions, organizational and business infighting, lawsuits, children's behavior, social image, family disputes, emergencies, unexpected accidents and deaths, financial crisis, early retirement, natural disasters, physical or mental disabilities, impoverishment, etc. To relieve some of the harshness of reality, people find some relief in smoking, using alcohol in moderation, taking prescription drugs, using illegal drugs, engaging in frequent sex, eating between meals, drinking coffee, etc. all of which may offset some of the other long term harmful effects. Using these may actually extend the longevity of life rather than shorten it. We need to make a series of comparative studies to be able to determine whether these are as detrimental to health as those who abstain and have no release or outlet for their tensions, stress, and anxieties.

Random Thoughts from the Cosmos

Is God merely a stern judge or does He have a sense of humor?

Random Thoughts from the Cosmos

Love breeds jealousy
and
jealousy breeds hate.

Random Thoughts from the Cosmos

Life is so frustrating!
Once you get what you want, either you
don't want it any more or you want
something better.

Random Thoughts from the Cosmos

*If you can't be logical, perhaps it's
because you're short circuited
somewhere.*

Random Thoughts from the Cosmos

Sometimes the only way you can get people's attention is to ignore them.

Random Thoughts from the Cosmos

I would like to know you better. Please tell me, is that possible? Or are you like me — one of those people whose personality is so fragmented that you're not quite sure who you are?

Random Thoughts from the Cosmos

College profs seldom award an "A" for imagination and originality.

Random Thoughts from the Cosmos

The Bible tells you to love everyone, but the man or woman in your life may tell you to love everyone is to love no one.

Random Thoughts from the Cosmos

You are a mature and emotionally stable adult if no one can make you feel guilty about the things you have done in the past.

Random Thoughts from the Cosmos

One of the reasons I am so perfect is that I set my own standards. I just keep lowering them until I reach an attainable level.

Random Thoughts from the Cosmos

Whenever you have a problem you can't resolve, you start looking for either a bar or a church.

Random Thoughts from the Cosmos

Every answer proposes one or more new questions, so how are we ever going to arrive at ultimate truth?

Random Thoughts from the Cosmos

Never trust anyone who says he would never lie, cheat, or deceive you. He is too good to be true.

Random Thoughts from the Cosmos

Why are our politicians spreading all of this hysteria over drugs, tobacco, alcohol, and pornography? Are they just trying to protect its citizenry from their harmful side effects or do they have another motive in mind? Frankly, it's a diversionary tactic to get you to focus your attention on something other than rebuilding the highways, upkeep of our national parks, the immigration problem, education, adequate medical care, welfare reform, national defense, term limits, syndicated crime, and the economy. If politicians are so interested in the nation's youth and their health, they should figure out some way of providing a national health care program for all Americans. They pedal hysteria over drugs, tobacco, and alcohol to divert your attention away from the more serious issues confronting this nation — namely, survival.

Random Thoughts from the Cosmos

*Only by being critical of other people's
short comings do we find any
self-justification for our own.*

Random Thoughts from the Cosmos

*If all rules, regulations, morals, and laws
were fixed, final, and absolute, life
would be unbearable.*

Random Thoughts from the Cosmos

Don't tell me your troubles! I am trying so hard to be something other than a garbage collector.

Random Thoughts from the Cosmos

*The more things you fear and dislike,
the more likely you will become bored
with life.*

Random Thoughts from the Cosmos

The thing that intrigues me the most is the mystery shrouded in your silence.

Random Thoughts from the Cosmos

Why did Ford fail to get reelected to the presidency? Who wants a Ford once you have had a Lincoln? In other words, it was Nix-on Ford.

Random Thoughts from the Cosmos

If you have a firm grip on reality, don't hang on too tight, it might shake the living daylights out of you. You need an emotional buffer zone.

24

Random Thoughts from the Cosmos

*The best way to get love is to give love.
Be ever mindful of the needs and
concerns of others. Learn to express
gratitude for everything others do for
you.*

Random Thoughts from the Cosmos

If you aren't a winner, you can always justify losing on the basis that it was a much needed lesson. It was a good experience which you can use again should the opportunity arise.

Random Thoughts from the Cosmos

Let it be known that God heals no one. It is man's faith in God that is the healing force. The power of belief is awesome.

Random Thoughts from the Cosmos

Someone told me that I have no obligations to myself other than to be myself. What I want to know is, "Which self shall I be?"

Random Thoughts from the Cosmos

Whenever you meet someone who knows you better than you know yourself, you are subject to his power and control. Know thyself 'o man before thy venture out too far.

Random Thoughts from the Cosmos

If you were a dweller on the planet of Celesius, you would know you cannot separate the spiritual from the material — for you see, all material manifestations are the products of unseen and invisible forces.

Random Thoughts from the Cosmos

*Dancing, probably next to sexual
intercourse, is one of the most
therapeutic physical and psychological
outlets for relief from frustrations,
anxieties, and the pressures of daily
living.*

Random Thoughts from the Cosmos

If you wait until retirement to do your thing, you may find out that you have forgotten how; your strength and energy may have become depleted; you may no longer be able to afford it; the government may have confiscated your social security; or you may find it too late to learn. So you better find the time and the money to do your thing now.

Random Thoughts from the Cosmos

If we believe in the free-enterprise system, why don't we allow the owner of a restaurant, coffee shop, bar, tavern, or night club to decide whether he will permit smoking in his own business establishment? Here is a typical example of having the government tell you how to run your business. If you don't like tobacco smoke, find a place which will meet your specifications. Give people a choice. If you don't like the food or service, you don't have to go back. If you want to go skiing, go hunting, drive a car, own a gun, or play football, should I forbid you to do so because you might get seriously injured or kill yourself? After all, I'm not only trying to protect you from yourself but the rest of society as well. All of these laws and ordinances are enough to drive a man to drink or rebel against the establishment.

Random Thoughts from the Cosmos

Boredom arises out of the excessive
usage of the words:
"don't"
"won't"
"can't"
"afraid"
and
"maybe."

Random Thoughts from the Cosmos

They say that there is no hope for the satisfied man. But then the question arises, "What hope is there for anyone who isn't satisfied?"

Random Thoughts from the Cosmos

There should be a law that states:
"Whenever you pass a law or ordinance,
you have to repeal one."

Random Thoughts from the Cosmos

Can you imagine sitting in a bar, tavern, or night club for a couple of hours inhaling secondary tobacco smoke while accepting the belief that secondary tobacco smoke is a greater threat to your health and life than the alcohol being consumed? You can hardly wait to get a sniff of the brown-cloud polluted air outside to escape from all the cigarette smoke inside. Don't give it a second thought that you might kill some innocent party while driving home feeling so self-righteous and smug about being a nonsmoker. Talk about hysteria created by a right-wing-propagandist coalition backed with big bucks, shows how easy it is to brainwash people. And then they allow people to vote on a nonsmoking bill in Boulder, Co., who never even step inside a drinking establishment. Don't try to tell me I live in a free country.

Random Thoughts from the Cosmos

Since most illnesses are caused by fear, guilt, anxiety, family finances, negative attitudes and erroneous beliefs, physicians only treat symptoms and never causes.

Random Thoughts from the Cosmos

The biggest job of the self-righteous is now behind them. They have pretty much squelched tobacco smoking. They have managed to ban it from public places, restaurants, bars, and night clubs. Now the next big assignment will be the prohibition on alcohol. Then after that, the next big item on the moral agenda will be the censorship of books, magazines, movies, and television. Let's make our reality into a fantasy world devoid of strife and conflict by either killing or imprisoning all the bad guys so we can devote all of our time to the worship of Jesus Christ and God. What shall I buy the children for Christmas? Most male children will ask for toy guns and weapons of mass destruction.

Random Thoughts from the Cosmos

Beware of the man who boasts that he doesn't drink, smoke, lie, cheat, steal, or is unfaithful to his spouse, for he will more likely than not end up trying to con you out of your last dollar or else he will insist that you drop it in the church collection plate.

Random Thoughts from the Cosmos

*Earth can't be all bad. If you rearrange the letters in the word **earth**, you get the word **heart**. Supposedly, it is love that makes the heart palpitate at an irregular beat. Strange that we should associate the heart with love when it is a mind trip.*

Random Thoughts from the Cosmos

Freud was a fraud. Self-preservation is a greater determinant of human behavior than the sex drive.

Random Thoughts from the Cosmos

*Nothing shocks me anymore. Most of
my friends have exhausted nearly all the
possibilities.*

Random Thoughts from the Cosmos

To be overly cautious is to deprive yourself of a totally enjoyable experience. What is life without a few calculated risks?

Random Thoughts from the Cosmos

When people state they are knowledgeable about religious or philosophical truths, they simply are not telling you the truth. In delineating truth, we have two major problems: semantics (meaning of words) and how we perceive phenomenon based upon our education and personal experiences. Perhaps it is good for the ego to make others believe that we are knowledgeable about truth even though we have some serious doubts about what it is ourselves. If we can get others to accept our truths as being the ultimate word of God, then those truths must be true, for how could God possibly allow such misconceptions to persist?

Random Thoughts from the Cosmos

To control others, for whatever selfish reasons you might have, requires that you relinquish that control periodically. It is the type of philosophy which implies: "I'll play your game if you'll play mine."

Random Thoughts from the Cosmos

*There are those who have a dependency
need to be rescued or saved, and then
there are those who feel it is their
mission in life to save an alcoholic or
win a soul to Christ.*

Random Thoughts from the Cosmos

Philosophy is the systematic and analytical study of inductive and deductive reasoning in an effort to prove a point, which generally ends up contradicting the very premise which one had hoped to confirm.

Random Thoughts from the Cosmos

A religion based on faith has no right to condemn those who seriously question some of the teachings in the Bible for there is no scientific evidence to support Christian dogma. Faith is the weakest link in helping man to understand who he is and the origin of his species. Those who claim that faith is a justifiable basis for imposing their beliefs or mores upon the rest of society is surely playing some dangerous games with people's minds. Acceptance by faith alone is the lazy man's way of coping and will lead to the enslavement of the human mind whereby man will ultimately lose his ability to think logically and solve complex problems.

Random Thoughts from the Cosmos

Have you ever heard of a minister who would publicly debate the authenticity of the Bible with a college professor of philosophy? The minister would surely be humiliated since the college professor who has studied the Bible as philosophy or literature could raise some rather interesting questions. Sooner or later, the minister would entrap himself in paradoxes, contradictions, and dichotomies. Don't ever expect to see or hear such a debate transpire here in the U.S.A. Even if there were one, it wouldn't get any media attention. Christians have considerable control over the publication and broadcasting industries. To find a major publisher for this book will not be an easy task.

Random Thoughts from the Cosmos

If there were no truths, wouldn't man be obliged to invent some in order to explain the unexplainable? After all, we need truths in order to maintain social order or some semblance of control over those rebellious souls who have asked some very disturbing questions or who have pointed out some rather obvious contradictions in the scriptures.

Random Thoughts from the Cosmos

You exclude from reality that which is of little or no interest to you. You observe and perceive what you want to observe and perceive, hear only what you want to hear, and know only what you want to know. That's leaving an awful lot out of the total picture. Your unwillingness to perceive and acknowledge only what you want to perceive and acknowledge may come back to haunt you some day after it is too late to change some of your beliefs and opinions.

Random Thoughts from the Cosmos

*If man has free will, how come he keeps
making the same mistakes over and over
again? What difference does it make
whether the mistake is of his own choice
or just allowed to happen in a relaxed,
casual, and leave-it-to-chance manner.
Man's choices are determined by forces
and conditions outside of his ability to
control them. Man might have lived a
happier existence and done a better job
managing his life had he never accepted
any belief in free will. That way, he
would quit worrying about the future.
There are very few people whoever had
dreams and plans whoever saw them
materialize as visualized. If there is such
a thing as free will, it would appear
some people have more choices than
others.*

Random Thoughts from the Cosmos

Some have said, "If I thought I didn't have any free will, I would kill myself or I would simply quit trying to better myself." No you wouldn't! It would only make you more determined than ever to prove the philosophy of determinism to be wrong as you refuse to accept such an unconscionable belief. Unfortunately, many who thought they had free will went bankrupt and are now destitute — especially those who thought that God was on their side; but the way things turned out, God was evidently on the side of the enemy or their competitors. In that event, one would have to wonder whether or not there is a God.

Random Thoughts from the Cosmos

Some philosophers say that the nice thing about believing in predestination is that everybody is doing precisely what they are supposed to be doing. Thus, we can quit condemning everyone for what they do and truly love them. Everyone is playing his or her designated role in life just as you are playing yours. We have to assume that everyone is doing the best he or she knows how under the circumstances and with whatever mental, physical, and financial resources at their disposal.

Random Thoughts from the Cosmos

One of the main criticisms of democracy is the amount of red tape you have in order to get anything done, which is to say nothing about bureaucratic waste. Red tape is one of the main stays of the legal profession and special interest groups. Special interest organizations have the country so bogged down in legal maneuvering that progress is stymied; but for all of that, the U.S.A. still has one of the best systems for governing. After all, if there wasn't something to fix, our politicians wouldn't know what to do with themselves.

Random Thoughts from the Cosmos

After God created Adam and Eve in the Garden of Eden, He had some misgivings about the whole affair. After watching them partake of all the things which He hath provided, He thought to Himself, "They will become bored with all the good things in life, man and woman need challenges." After thinking about the problem for a few minutes, God summoned the serpent to the royal court at which time He issued a formal proclamation: "And now, let the games begin."

Random Thoughts from the Cosmos

*Consult a failure. He may have more
insight into why he failed than the
successful man has into why he
succeeded. The successful man (woman)
may have been too busy to stop and
analyze his methods and techniques or to
teach them to others. Why should he
share them with others when he might
just be creating more competition for
himself?*

Random Thoughts from the Cosmos

Some couples spat merely to have something to say to one another. Whenever two people agree on a topic, the conversation is generally over. Fighting, like mating, is frequently nothing more than some type of ritualistic communication even though it may appear to be much more devastating and serious. No one likes to be a "yes" man all the time.

Random Thoughts from the Cosmos

If we can't find happiness why should anyone else? Maybe we can balance things out a little by trying to make others just as miserable as ourselves merely because we can't stand the thought of others having something we haven't got. As long as we are afflicted and oftentimes obsessed with jealousy, resentment, vindictiveness, bitterness, and envy toward nonconformists, we have our attention focused on the negative. Under those conditions, there is little likelihood we will ever find peace of mind and inner contentment.

Random Thoughts from the Cosmos

Whether one makes correct moral or ethical choices is largely dependent on one's respect for those authorities who set the standards for social behavior and whether these law makers (be they political or ecclesiastical) personally adhere to the rules, laws, and commandments which they advocate for others. Hypocrisy creates rebellion especially among adolescents. Kids scrutinize adult behavior more than society is willing to acknowledge. They see all the sham and pretense in the games being played in the business, social, and church worlds.

Random Thoughts from the Cosmos

What we call thinking is more or less a stimulus and reflex response. If and when you think, answers are not always at the tip of your tongue. Thinking requires concentration, deliberation, and some imagination. It can be a time-consuming and mentally-exhausting process. Unfortunately, most people don't have the time or else they are unwilling to try. It is too easy to watch TV or read a novel.

Random Thoughts from the Cosmos

Life is a series of experiments which we call experiences. By the time we have been able to formulate any conclusions and to modify our thinking, personality, and behavior, either we are too old or we have found it more comfortable to merely accept things the way they are.

Random Thoughts from the Cosmos

Nearly everyone plays games. Those who are unaware of the games they are playing and lose may become bitter and neurotic. Those who play games consciously and deliberately will take their losses in stride knowing that life is playing the percentages and that you can't win 'em all.

Random Thoughts from the Cosmos

Why should I lie to you? I am espousing truths which were told to me by my parents, teachers, and the clergy, which have been hand-me downs for hundreds of years through countless generations. But I can't help wondering if they could have believed anything other than what they were told since that's all they were ever exposed to. Any new thought or idea was clearly the work of the devil.

Random Thoughts from the Cosmos

As far as the politicians we send to Washington, I would just as soon pay them to do nothing because whatever they do merely complicates matters making them even worse. Provide them with enough sex, booze, and parties; then maybe, they'll quit disrupting the status quo. I can't seem to adapt to change as fast as they can pass legislation.

Random Thoughts from the Cosmos

No gospel can be translated from one language to another without something being lost in the translation. If we cannot even agree on what words mean in our own language, how can we be so absolutely certain as to what words mean which have been interpreted hundreds of times by Biblical scholars from as many different languages for nearly two thousand years. God help us if such scholars ever injected any of their own thoughts, ideas, and beliefs into their translations.

Random Thoughts from the Cosmos

Be ye not concerned over the money spent on welfare programs. No money gets back into circulation faster than that spent by social security and welfare recipients. Don't fret over such a trivial matter. It ultimately finds its way back to the top of the economic ladder by those who paid the taxes in the first place. Without that income, businessmen would not be nearly as well off as they are now. Contrary to what many believe, money does not trickle down to the very poor. Excessive profits and low income taxes are being used to play the markets — which is nothing more than buying and selling money.

We are flirting with a financial disaster.

Random Thoughts from the Cosmos

Winners are those who reminisce about the times and occasions when they have won. Happy people reminisce about the times when they were happy. Losers reminisce about the times they've lost. Unhappy people reminisce about the times they were unhappy. Some can't recall much of anything. Winning, losing, happiness, and unhappiness are all states of consciousness.

Why does Judaism appear to be a more materialistic religion than Christianity? Could it be because most sects of the Hebrew religion do not embrace any belief in the immortality of the human soul? Without fear of punishment for one's sins and transgressions, moral and ethical conduct is solely regulated by statutory laws or fear of expulsion from the church by a governing hierarchy. If there is no afterlife why should one be concerned about morals and ethics? Of course Christians don't have to be concerned with morals or ethics because once you're saved in the name of the Lord you are always saved.

Random Thoughts from the Cosmos

Do you really think it is possible to inhale enough tobacco smoke in a restaurant, bar, or night club for the short time you are in one — an hour or two — to develop lung cancer? It might be possible if you had to live or work in a concentrated-smoke-filled room more than eight hours a day. It is surprising the number of people who grew up with a parent or parents who smoked and who later smoked themselves none of whom died of a tobacco related illness. And what about all the pollution you breathe after you leave the parameters of your home, office, restaurant or bar which evidently is of little concern to nonsmokers? Aren't we being somewhat paranoid over the inherent dangers of secondary tobacco smoke when the air outside, which you have to breathe 24 hours a day, contains far more dangerous particulates than the smoke inside?

Random Thoughts from the Cosmos

You are most likely to be taken in by some silver-tongued orator, politician, priest, or minister when everything in life has suddenly taken a turn for the worse, and you seemingly cannot cope any longer. Once you relinquish control of your mind to someone else who tells you how to live your life and what to believe, you are in just as much trouble, if not greater, than you were before, and you have given much of your time and money to someone or an institution that can't do all that much for you.

Random Thoughts from the Cosmos

Are you looking and waiting for happiness to suddenly appear out of nowhere? Some are waiting for the clouds to part and with a clap of thunder, some strange mysterious, and ecstatic feeling will overwhelm them with joy and happiness. Most are disappointed at life's end waiting for a miracle to happen. How are you going to find happiness if you don't have a few preconceived ideas as to precisely what it would take to make you happy? Some goals are necessary and vital to your pursuit of happiness.

Random Thoughts from the Cosmos

Some ingredients for success are:
desire
goals
organization
knowledge
experience
talents
personality
perseverance
confidence
assertiveness
discipline
confidence
good health
and
proper mental attitude.

Random Thoughts from the Cosmos

Each human is a different vial of chemistry. Now if earth is bombarded with cosmic rays, and they are capable of penetrating the human body, then the chemical reaction is going to be different in each person. Blending of individual chemistry with cosmic energy creates a new synthetic chemistry which can effect human behavior causing moodiness and changeability. If common drugs affect human behavior then cosmic radiations can do likewise. Even the soil under our feet gives off residual-radiational energy — some of it's good and some is bad. Some people would do better by moving to a new locale.

Random Thoughts from the Cosmos

Unless you can translate and convert money from dollars and cents into feelings and emotions of well-being, there is little incentive to make anything more than a mere living.

Get comfortable, relax, and visualize a time, a place, and the condition which would give you the greatest joy, pleasure, serenity, and happiness possible.

Projection and visualization are vital steps to making the dollars needed for fulfilling your dreams and goals.

Random Thoughts from the Cosmos

Are UFO occupants outer-space visitors or merely curious spectators? Why should beings from other planets or dimensions get involved with earthlings? In what way could we contribute to their intelligence or knowledge? They are probably evolved enough to know that possession and occupancy of the earth would entail a responsibility they would not care to assume. After all, if they needed more space, they possess the technical knowledge to create a synthetic planet more suitable to their needs. They are intelligent enough to know that wars resolve nothing, and they would like to convey this message back to the inhabitants of planet Earth.

Random Thoughts from the Cosmos

*If some man claimed that he was God,
what greater proof would one need than
to accuse him of fraud and place him on
the cross knowing that if he were truly
God, he would have no trouble
extricating himself without wounds or
scars? Christ died on the cross, but his
resurrection was witnessed by no one.
How embarrassing for poor Judas when
he discovered that Christ failed to
demonstrate publicly that he was the
Godhead. Poor Judas hung himself out
of disillusionment when he found out
that Christ was but a man who could
not escape the tortures of being
crucified. Christ had the multitudes to
witness his ascension if he had chosen
to do so. Even the skeptics would have
been convinced.*

Random Thoughts from the Cosmos

Please explain why some people take an almost immediate and compulsive interest in some study, hobby, or creative expression when they have never been subjected to brainwashing or being exposed to the subject matter previously. Is it strictly a matter of genes or could it be some type of psychic residue carried over from a previous lifetime? Genes provide us with the necessary skills, while the human mind produces the necessary desire and knowledge.

Random Thoughts from the Cosmos

Every angel has an angle.

Random Thoughts from the Cosmos

Happiness is having patient creditors.

Random Thoughts from the Cosmos

One is about as honest and truthful as one dares to be.

Random Thoughts from the Cosmos

Happiness is abandoning the ship before it sinks.

Random Thoughts from the Cosmos

I would like to be perfect, but I never found anyone to show me how.

Random Thoughts from the Cosmos

You can always go out and cause trouble when society and law enforcement prohibits you from doing the things you find pleasurable or when you're seeking relief from the stress and strain caused by a highly controlled society. You don't have to go out and sit in a bar and get drunk. You can always stay home and watch sports or live in a fantasy world by watching movies of fictional sex and violence on television. Please don't watch the news — that's for real. You could turn to a religious channel in which some tele-evangelist will tell you what a really bad person you are. Instead, why not go out somewhere? Go skiing, to a fancy restaurant, to the theater, or take a short vacation where you can do things you would never think of doing at home (like Las Vegas). "Too poor," you say. "Then stay at home and smoke your damn cigarettes, drink your beer, and spend the evening fantasizing

Random Thoughts from the Cosmos

watching television. See if I care. I can't help it if you haven't enough money. You should have chosen another career or taken another path. I have no empathy for you. You made your bed now lie in it. And don't tell me it's destiny. Anybody can make it big that halfway tries." "But sir," I said, "Why are you so hostile? You either must be terribly unhappy or have a guilty conscience."

Random Thoughts from the Cosmos

Unless people are willing to change, good counsel goes for naught.

Random Thoughts from the Cosmos

The most gratifying recognition comes from knowledge and solid achievement rather than by deceiving and manipulating people.

Random Thoughts from the Cosmos

Whenever the sex drive starts to diminish, good food and booze seem to take on added importance.

Random Thoughts from the Cosmos

Adam and Eve thought they were in pair-a-dice until they were confronted with snake eyes.

Random Thoughts from the Cosmos

A conformist is one who finds it necessary to play games in order to survive.

Random Thoughts from the Cosmos

Happiness is remembering the fun we've had while we are now paying for it.

Random Thoughts from the Cosmos

*When God created the first man and
woman, He should have named them
Adam and Even.*

Random Thoughts from the Cosmos

*What is a liberal? A liberal is anyone
who isn't a conservative. But what is a
conservative? He is anyone who isn't a
liberal. What is a left-wing libertarian?
Who knows? We are identified by a
whole lot of labels which are not of our
choosing. Labels can be a means of
attempting to describe who we are by
those who know us the least. There are
liberal Republicans and conservative
Democrats. It's no wonder the world is
so messed up. Labels are the tools of
propagandists used to arouse emotions.
It takes the media, a preacher, or a
politician to define those labels, but I'm
not even sure there is total unanimity
among themselves as to what those
terms mean.*

Random Thoughts from the Cosmos

Truth may be found in churches, bars, and coffee shops. Truth is whatever you can make anyone believe it is.

Random Thoughts from the Cosmos

To be perfect would require 90% more effort merely to achieve another 10%. It simply isn't worth it.

Random Thoughts from the Cosmos

It takes more than positive thinking to win a gold medal in the Olympics. It takes talent and natural ability just for openers. Any number of participants who "thought positive" and "visualized winning" in their meditations came home empty handed. But how many of those medal winners discovered that the price for glory wasn't worth it as they neglected other facets of their lives? So who was the winner and who was the loser? Isn't there some satisfaction in knowing that you gave it your best shot? Compare the winners with the losers thirty years later and you may get a new perspective on who the real winners and losers were.

Random Thoughts from the Cosmos

Happiness is dramatizing your point in an effort to make a big deal over practically nothing.

Random Thoughts from the Cosmos

If someone mistreats you, you should look within yourself for the possible causes.

Random Thoughts from the Cosmos

*Repentance is something you can do
when everything you have done fails,
goes amiss, and starts backfiring.*

Random Thoughts from the Cosmos

It is every man's dream to get something in excess of the time, money, and effort he puts into his endeavors and goals.

Random Thoughts from the Cosmos

Bar Room Openers

You are probably not my type but I can't always tell; nonetheless, I'm open to experimentation. Maybe a new experience would be good for me.

🐏 🐏 🐏

Don't I know you? Sure, now I remember! You were my mistress in a previous life. I'm sorry about having to kill you. I lost my head when I found out you were cheating on me. Please forgive me! But look, here we are — alive and well. You look great for having been dead so long. Little did I ever expect to see you again. I guess, it's time that I apologize and try to make some amends. May I start by buying you a drink?

Random Thoughts from the Cosmos

Some people are absolutely petrified, terrified, and/or paralyzed when they hear or see anything which makes them aware of the possibility that there just might be other alternatives and beliefs never before considered. You can't help but feel sorry for them when they are exposed to something contrary to what they have believed and clung to forever so many years. Sometimes it takes a tragedy or disaster to make them receptive to some new ideas or philosophy of life.

Random Thoughts from the Cosmos

Losers go around trying to convince others that winning isn't everything.

Random Thoughts from the Cosmos

Sanity is sitting on the sidelines observing life. Insanity is getting involved.

Random Thoughts from the Cosmos

If you are looking for answers, ask the guy or gal sitting on the adjacent bar stool. They are more than willing to set you straight.

Random Thoughts from the Cosmos

To have a good marriage or partnership there needs to be one dominant party and the other submissive. Two domineering bosses will never make it.

Random Thoughts from the Cosmos

As long as people think you know something that they don't know and it might be worth knowing, they will be more than willing to play your game.

Random Thoughts from the Cosmos

Admit that I am wrong! I would rather lie to you first, make excuses, or blame someone else. After all it is necessary to protect what little "ego" I have left.

Random Thoughts from the Cosmos

People who preach tolerance often become intolerant of those who are intolerant and biased against those who are biased.

Random Thoughts from the Cosmos

What's your concept as to what life is all about? Don't forget to include in your statement:

Sex
Work
&
Taxes

Random Thoughts from the Cosmos

Of course, there are certain questions which psychologists and philosophers, like their ministerial brethren, are unwilling to answer. How can idiot savants be classified as idiots or morons and, yet, perform certain talents and abilities that most geniuses can't even perform? Some children seem to develop certain artistic talents early in their lives with very little effort. Did they have these abilities prior to birth? Why haven't these questions been addressed by those who claim to know everything about man and God? Probably, it's because the ministry and the social scientists have already ruled out the possibility that reincarnation is a viable answer. Perhaps they should read some of the hundreds of books written and published on occult subjects.

Random Thoughts from the Cosmos

Since God is such a stern judge, I much prefer a jury. Besides, hasn't He got anything better to do than to pass judgement on the likes of me? After all, He has the entire universe to manage and control.

Random Thoughts from the Cosmos

*Envy, jealousy, greed, lying, cheating,
stealing, deceiving and hate are just as
destructive as obesity, guns, alcoholism,
drugs, and smoking. The tangible sins
are more readily identifiable than the
intangible. But if there is a God, He
surely knows the difference between
what we are and what we try to appear
before our peers.*

Random Thoughts from the Cosmos

*If you want to discover another facet of
reality which you have never had the
opportunity to discover or explore, start
associating with people who do not share
all of your preconceived ideas and beliefs
about things.*

Random Thoughts from the Cosmos

For many who are trying to find out what life is all about, the more you tell them that something is evil or sinful, the more they want to experience it to find out why it is so appealing. Part of one's childhood should be the right to experiment without the fear of being sent to prison or jail for some unjustifiable and unreasonable period of time.

Random Thoughts from the Cosmos

After awhile, when you tire of gossiping about others, you may decide it would be more exciting to be gossiped about. After all, why should all of your friends be the center of attention?

Random Thoughts from the Cosmos

*Who wants **ordinary** common sense? Isn't there something above and beyond ordinary? How about **extraordinary** or, maybe, even **extra-sensory perception**? How about cosmic vibrations which manifest in instantaneous knowledge without ever having to learn it by attending school, taking a course, or learning it through experience? How do people write a fiction book in which ideas and words flow effortlessly between the mind and the pen, typewriter, or word processor? It is so spontaneous and automatic that it doesn't even require thinking. You may be getting some assistance from the spirit world.*

Random Thoughts from the Cosmos

If you can't love me the way I am, at least show me a little mercy, love, and compassion. Just remember I got programmed in the same haphazard manner as you did.

Random Thoughts from the Cosmos

I spend so much of my time rationalizing my mistakes, justifying my actions, and passing the buck that I have little or no time for more constructive-type games.

Random Thoughts from the Cosmos

Winners are losers who keep on trying. They not only profit from their own mistakes, but also from observing the techniques and mistakes of those who are better than they are. You may also learn from the mistakes of those who were failures if you wanted to pursue that possibility — especially if they had been successful for a number of years before they started on the downward slide.

Random Thoughts from the Cosmos

*Without some fantasies and illusions,
life would be unbearable. The interesting
thing is that some of them actually come
to pass — with some pretty bizarre
endings too.*

Random Thoughts from the Cosmos

If it appears I am somewhat egotistical, it's because I am one of the world's foremost authorities on: "the games people have no damn business playing."

Random Thoughts from the Cosmos

Movies, newspapers, novels, and short stories evolve mostly around sex and violence. If the sex drive is thwarted for any sustained period of time, it may well erupt into some form of violence or antisocial behavior. Perhaps prostitution would be instrumental in stemming the tide in both domestic violence and the high incidence of rape. Everyone needs some type of escapist activity as a release from frustrations, anxiety, tension, reversals, disappointments, and unfulfilled desires. Sex can be likened to a relief valve on a pressure cooker.

Random Thoughts from the Cosmos

*If you want to be the hit of the party,
talk about someone other than yourself.*

Random Thoughts from the Cosmos

If you were the only girl and I was the only boy left on planet earth, would you still insist that it had to be done your way or not at all?

Random Thoughts from the Cosmos

Why does God need my love? He has everything He needs already. If He needs my love, He has the power to change me.

Random Thoughts from the Cosmos

*Woman was appropriately named as she brought **<u>woe to man</u>** or it might have been because she said, "**<u>Whoa man</u>**! What in the hell are you trying to pull, anyway?"*

Random Thoughts from the Cosmos

Politicians, physicians, lawyers, psychologists, psychiatrists, preachers, and priests have a common cross to bear. They really have no way of knowing with any degree of certainty whether or not they can deliver what they promised.

Random Thoughts from the Cosmos

If you don't like yourself the way you are, you could learn to play games. In fact, if you feel the necessity for change and improvement, you are going to have to start thinking and behaving quite unnaturally.

Random Thoughts from the Cosmos

Experience is a great teacher, but most of the lessons we have learned, we will probably never have the opportunity to use again. No matter how old we get we are always confronted with new and different problems. It's unfortunate that someone else couldn't profit from our mistakes since there is little likelihood that we will ever encounter a similar situation again. Our earlier experiences, however, may have taught us to be a little more cautious and methodical in the planning stages of any new venture.

Random Thoughts from the Cosmos

Some young people get married because they seek a new experience, and they're curious and anxious to see what life holds in store for them. However, the only thing they are prepared to accept is nothing short of sheer bliss.

Random Thoughts from the Cosmos

One spends so much of his life keeping up appearances, earning a living, maintaining property, and keeping track of one's tax deductions, that one has little or no time to associate with those who might share his creative and intellectual interests.

Random Thoughts from the Cosmos

*Matthew 22:37 "Jesus said unto him,
Thou shalt love the Lord thy God with
all thy heart, and all thy soul, and all
thy mind. This is the first and greatest
commandment. And the second is like
unto it. Thou shalt love thy neighbor as
thyself. On these two commandments
hang all the law and the prophets." Now
what I want to know is: suppose your
neighbor*
*• is a homosexual • is an exconvict
• smokes pot • uses bad language
• doesn't keep his yard up to
neighborhood standards • tells dirty
jokes • is an atheist • uses drugs • is an
alcoholic • has long hair • his kids are
troublemakers (or) live on
welfare — then what?*
*Surely, there must be some exceptions to
Biblical law.*

Random Thoughts from the Cosmos

A path is something people seek in an effort to discover truth and happiness. Once they are on the so-called path, they never stray from it until it becomes a well-worn rut — a rut which they can't see over the top or climb out of. It never occurred to them that there may be more than one pathway leading to enlightenment and happiness.

Random Thoughts from the Cosmos

Nearly everyone has some expertise in one or two departments of life. Most of us have some talents or abilities to excel at something which surfaces briefly from time to time. If you haven't found yours as yet, it's because it is playing hide and seek in some dark and unexplored region of your subconscious mind. It wouldn't hurt if you were to try a little Zen meditation.

Random Thoughts from the Cosmos

A man who does things on impulse
occasionally may live a longer and
happier life. He may reject the theory
that impulsiveness always leads to chaos
or disaster. Sometimes impulsiveness
turns out to be quite rewarding,
pleasurable, and relaxing. What one may
call impulsiveness others call intuition.

Random Thoughts from the Cosmos

God is often portrayed as an old man, with a long white beard, and dressed in a white robe. He may have fooled everyone, however, for He shaved off his beard, wears conventional clothes, was born of a natural mother, drives an old Volvo, smokes when no one is looking, and is a womanizer. He has had many different vocations, and is classified as a drifter. He has been seen sitting on the banks of the Mississippi near Clinton, Iowa possibly contemplating what He might do differently if He had the opportunity to do it all over again. Almost everybody has talked to him or seen him, but no two people seem to agree as to what he looks like. Apparently it is impossible to see through his disguises.

Random Thoughts from the Cosmos

Why ministers and priests condemn poor Judas of Iscariot for betraying Christ is not easily understood. Don't they realize there wouldn't even be a Christian religion or the ministry have a job, if it weren't for the much maligned Judas? Judas was just playing the role he was predestined to play in this Cosmic drama. Perhaps he will, if he has not already, reincarnate to settle an old score for being set up as the fall guy. I'm sure he is most anxious to clear his name as being a willful participant in the crucifixion of Christ. For you see, God orchestrated the entire event. He chose the script, designed the setting, directed, produced, and chose the actors.

Random Thoughts from the Cosmos

It seems almost paradoxical that some of the happiest people are the most bigoted and biased, who have definite beliefs about everything under the sun. Where they got these beliefs without going to a seminary or learning them formally in college is beyond me. Such is their state of bliss until their offspring moves away from home or goes to college and then comes back home to challenge their parents' ideas, beliefs, and values. These proteges may even reject their parent's beliefs and values as a valid base for happiness.

Random Thoughts from the Cosmos

If National Health Care is such an inferior grade of medical care, please explain these statistics. Longevity of life for males and females in different countries which have national health plans are:

	Male	Female
Australia	74	80
Canada	74	81
Denmark	72	78
Finland	72	80
France	74	82
Israel	76	79
Norway	74	81
Sweden	75	81
United States*	72	79

Does not have national care.

Random Thoughts from the Cosmos

Infant mortality per 1,000 live births is:

Australia	8
Canada	7.3
Denmark	7
Finland	6
France	7
Israel	9
Norway	11
Sweden	11
United States	10

These statistics were taken from the 1994 edition of the <u>World Almanac</u>.

Random Thoughts from the Cosmos

Some people keep playing the same, old worn-out records over and over again in their minds with the same negative refrains. These mind recordings become so obsessive that there is little opportunity for anything positive to assert itself. Hate, resentment, disappointment, anger, jealousy, and low self-esteem take their toll among the masses, creating serious and adverse effects on physical and mental health.

Random Thoughts from the Cosmos

To control your destiny, you must first learn to control your emotions and feelings. Once you have mastered the technique, you may then learn to control others long enough to allow them to do for you what you want. The question is not whether one should control and manipulate others, but a question relative to methods and degrees.

Random Thoughts from the Cosmos

Frequently psychiatrists and psychologists have been known to relieve their clients of fears and guilt by neutralizing their beliefs. They deprogram them without reprogramming them. Beliefs and values should be replaced by other beliefs and values. Most of us like to play the role of a counselor or psychologist, but we should be careful about destroying another's religion or beliefs unless we have something to offer which could make a difference in their pursuit for security and happiness.

Random Thoughts from the Cosmos

Some would say put the past behind you and forget it. But without some time to reminisce and without memories, life would be a useless experience. It is rather unfortunate, but few of us have had the occasion to recall our earlier experiences. Diaries, scrap books, photo albums, and home movies and videos are good memory joggers. There really is nothing wrong with living in the past as long as you're happy doing so and have some fond recollections. In fact, it is much cheaper to live in the past than in the present because you are content to stay at home and reminisce about the good old days. Just think how entertaining it might be if we had video taped our lives.

Random Thoughts from the Cosmos

Comedians and humorists are needed throughout the world, but how can you trust someone who isn't serious all the time? Comedians, as a lot, try to call your attention to some disturbing events in our world by trivializing their seriousness. They make you laugh when you feel like crying. On the other hand, I am suspicious of people who lack a sense of humor. They seem too intense on getting their fair share of the world's wealth. There is a growing segment of our population which is so solemn, they simply can't be trusted.

Random Thoughts from the Cosmos

Some say they live by the Bible, but the Bible has contrasting philosophies by which you can live. Do you live by the "eye-for-an-eye" philosophy of the Old Testament or by the "turn-the-other-cheek" philosophy in the New Testament? The Old Testament says there are ten commandments but Jesus says there are but two. Christ came to offer the world a new dispensation, so why are we bogged down by the teachings of the Old Testament?

Random Thoughts from the Cosmos

The evolution of the human soul does not call for isolation from the world but calls for getting out and getting involved. Chances are you're going to get involved with someone who is going to cause you more grief than you ever bargained for.

But it is these negative experiences which enhance soul growth. Perhaps, in your next life you won't remember your current experiences, but they may have a profound effect upon your decision-making processes. Possibly, in the life to follow, your subconscious mind will remind you to play your cards with a little more skill and finesse.

Random Thoughts from the Cosmos

Why all this interest in the occult, metaphysics, and mysticism? Most of the major religions in the world started in cultures where transportation centered around animals or animal-drawn vehicles. Why should one be bogged down with an oxcart religion in an era characterized by machines, self-propelled vehicles, and space-age technology?

Random Thoughts from the Cosmos

One can generally trust his sensory impressions and logic until he watches a master magician perform. One may then become aware that either reality is an illusion or the magician and his tricks are. One reason that some truly gifted magicians can't tell you how they perform their tricks, is there is nothing to tell. Is it just one of those miraculous gifts which no one, not even yourself, would believe even if you were told the truth? Could he have hypnotized us to believe he did something he actually never did? Is he performing certain actions or manipulations in a sequence the so-called mind cannot logically perceive?

Random Thoughts from the Cosmos

The Bible says, "Let the dead bury the dead." Perhaps that is not as far fetched as people might think. Some appear to be alive, but are mentally, spiritually, and socially dead. They are totally oblivious as to what is going on around them. Many among us are dead because some member of the clergy made them fearful of the wrath of God or laid some guilt trips on them making them feel unworthy as members of the human race. Thus, they are unable to think or reason things out logically. What we don't use, we lose, and that applies to those who accept Biblical scriptures on faith without taking note of its discrepancies and inconsistencies.

Random Thoughts from the Cosmos

Some Christians maintain the Bible is infallible. I, personally, wouldn't know, but I am well aware of the fact the people who read and interpret it are not, and especially those who claim every word is literally true.

Random Thoughts from the Cosmos

Is earth a compatible environment for the human soul? Come! Let us respond to this challenge. If we all pitch in, we could make it a more desirable place for those who have faith that it could be a paradise. Unfortunately, there is little opportunity for that to happen when we are told that paradise is a place where the soul migrates after death. Everyone talks about heaven, but nobody seems to be too eager to make the necessary sacrifices to find out. We want to cling to life, our families, and our wealth even though the ministry has portrayed heaven as an utopian paradise. When given a choice between life and death, most of us prefer life no matter what the church teaches.

Random Thoughts from the Cosmos

The self-righteous Christians who support legislation to enforce their moral precepts upon nonbelievers are enough to drive a man to drink or rebel against the established social order. Too many reforms and mandates create civil unrest and disobedience as boredom begins to manifest. These mandates and laws are not designed to solve social problems, but to impose restraints upon individual freedoms to prevent a minority from engaging in such activities which they find pleasurable or to escape the oppressiveness of a highly controlled society where everything is taboo or illegal. Alcohol and tobacco may be all the lower economic classes can afford to escape stress, anxiety, and the rigors of daily living, while the affluent can engage in any number of escapist activities which are socially acceptable. While the upper-middle class, the lower-upper class, and the wealthy want to prohibit others from using drugs, alcohol, and tobacco, they, in turn, may obtain by prescription, psychiatric drugs (Ritalin, Prozac, Zoloft, Lithium, Valium) which may be just as harmful as illegal drugs.

Random Thoughts from the Cosmos

Anxiety and frustration may be created by propaganda, industrialization, technology, religion, racism, social and economic classes, discrimination, environment, self-interests clashing with public interests, reformers, urbanization, coalitions, an aging citizenry, and overcrowded cities. These are problems for which sociologists have few, if any, solutions since they have little political input into the governing of this country. We have hit an impasse which may lead to total paralysis, chaos, and a revolution in which a dictator will emerge to assume the leadership of the country controlled by a one party system. Yes, there will be books burned and banned in the process. First we have to get rid of public radio.

Random Thoughts from the Cosmos

Is the real world the one you see with the naked eye or the one you see under a microscope? Suppose you haven't been trained or educated to observe the world from either perspective. Now superimpose upon reality your feelings, emotions, and opinions about things and people. Your initial impressions and the ones to follow may become so distorted that you are no longer in touch with reality. There are too many judgments based on appearances, insufficient knowledge, emotions, and other superficial criteria for one to be reality oriented.

Random Thoughts from the Cosmos

Is reality what you observed yesterday, or is it the one that you observed ten minutes ago, or is it the one you are observing this very minute? Not only the world has changed in that short time but your observation point has shifted with it. Another facet of the reality question is that we may have acquired some additional knowledge or information which would have changed the previous perceptions of what we had experienced earlier. What additional information and experiences are going to come later that will give us yet a different glimpse? Reality is not a static condition frozen in time or space.

Random Thoughts from the Cosmos

Quite frequently the man who gets criticized the most is the one most envied.

Random Thoughts from the Cosmos

One of the commandments states: "Thou shalt not commit murder." There are two types of murder, however, physical and psychological. The penalty for the physical is death or imprisonment. The psychological murderer is performed by those who tell you the earth is no damn good and unless you make a commitment to Christ, you are damned for the rest of eternity. Any man who even suggests this to be true is a con-artist. To live your life in strict compliance to God's will, is death for anyone lacking the means to think and analyze things for oneself. One is being groomed for the role of a robot.

Random Thoughts from the Cosmos

If God loves Christians more than anyone else why doesn't He protect his missionaries from the ravages of rape, murder, and tropical diseases in the jungles of South America and Africa? Why did so many sincere and honest devotees of Christ perish by the millions during two world wars? Interestingly enough, even some of the survivors, for some strange reason, still sing praises to God's goodness and greatness even though their countries were ravaged and their friends and families killed. Yes, He is all powerful when He denies man the ability to think and reason for himself only to render man a slave to the will of God.

Random Thoughts from the Cosmos

Personal Commentary

The author of this book had a daughter who died of cancer at the age of four. You may have had a relative die in an accident at the expense of a drunk driver. Based upon your feelings and emotions, the drunk driver should be executed or given a life sentence. So what do you do? You join MADD — the mothers or fathers against drunk drivers. So, let's take alcohol away from everyone. Based on your logic, I would like to see all churches closed because it was God who took my daughter's life and not some drunk driver. Could it be that "When it's your time, it's your time?" So why pin the blame on anyone if it is God's will? It was foreordained.

Random Thoughts from the Cosmos

Americans can no longer speak of their nation as a bastion of freedom. Freedom no longer exists in the U.S.A., for we have passed hundreds of ordinances restricting our rights to do things which seldom have any affect on anyone but oneself. I personally enumerated nearly two hundred rights which we no longer have but had thirty to forty years ago.

Trying to make the world safe for everyone is absurd. It simply can't be done. When man reaches the saturation point of being told what to think, how to behave, and what his moral and family values shall be, all of his pent-up emotions of frustration, anxiety, stress, and repressions will erupt causing riots, demonstrations, mayhem, and murder.

Random Thoughts from the Cosmos

Every time someone dies of a disease, is injured, or killed related to alcohol, tobacco, drugs, sex or abortion, we find it appropriate to look for new ways of curbing these so-called harmful activities. For instance, if one person is a fatality from just one of these causes, others will take it upon themselves to try and prohibit its usage even though it may have been the only harmful incident out of a thousand. You punish one person to prohibit 999 others from engaging in such activities, which they deem pleasurable. Most who use these substances are in complete control of themselves and their faculties. As long as we keep passing laws to protect people from themselves, it can no longer be said we are a free country.

Random Thoughts from the Cosmos

Jesus said, "Ye have heard that it hath been said, Thou shalt love thy neighbor and hate thine enemy. But I say unto you, Love your enemies, bless them that curse you, do good to them that hate you and pray for them which despitefully use you, and persecute you"—Matthew 5:43. Now the question arises, "Who is the enemy?" The enemy is anyone who tries to take away your freedom to say what you want to say, believe as you want to believe, or who supports legislation to make it illegal for you to enjoy something which is pleasurable or relaxing. The enemy, in the opinion of the majority, is usually a nonconformist who openly criticizes the social customs and mores of the times. Several decades from now all of that may have changed. You may be just a little ahead of your time. Of course, you could be declared a public nuisance for espousing your opinions and beliefs publicly to eyes who don't want to see or to ears who don't want to hear.

Random Thoughts from the Cosmos

You're O.K. as long as you think I am.

Random Thoughts from the Cosmos

If you can't love me the way I am, don't even bother.

Random Thoughts from the Cosmos

Boredom arises more often than not
when someone other than yourself
becomes the center of attention.

Random Thoughts from the Cosmos

Justice is not for all. It is only for those who can afford it.

Random Thoughts from the Cosmos

Politicians have definite beliefs and commitments prior to being elected to office, but readily change their minds if they believe they are supporting a bill which does not have the support of the people back home. As the political winds shift, so does their vote. There are very few jobs in the civilian world that can use a politician who just lost an election bid, so he tries to second guess what the majority of the voters want in an effort to retain his job. Most politicians embrace their party's philosophy, but when the going gets rough and they feel they no longer have the public's support, they will do a complete flip-flop. No one seems to have the courage of their convictions.

Random Thoughts from the Cosmos

Love is what you have left over after deducting all financial considerations.

Random Thoughts from the Cosmos

*People who measure success by dollars
and cents are frequently socially,
intellectually, emotionally, and
spiritually bankrupt.*

Random Thoughts from the Cosmos

If you love God, why shouldn't he love you? Why does he lay all of those heavy trips on you when you least need them?

Random Thoughts from the Cosmos

Winners cause things to happen. Losers sit around waiting for things to happen.

Random Thoughts from the Cosmos

God is not dead. He just abandoned an experiment that got completely out of hand.

Random Thoughts from the Cosmos

We are bombarded by propaganda constantly; and if we are blitzed long enough, we will accept suggestion as fact. Perhaps it is true that tobacco products are hazardous to your health, but are they anymore dangerous than eating between meals and being overweight? Comparing the abuse of tobacco with food, I would bet that those who use tobacco live longer than those who are compulsive eaters or who use alcoholic beverages. Drinking has greater social acceptance than smoking. For that matter, anything when done in excess may be detrimental to your health. Excessive hate probably will kill more people than secondary tobacco smoke. Caffeine is probably worse for you than wine.

Random Thoughts from the Cosmos

The only sane people are those who periodically question their own sanity.

Random Thoughts from the Cosmos

Sometimes we become so preoccupied with the mysteries of life, we forget to live life.

Random Thoughts from the Cosmos

Many fundamental preachers who damn the material things in life end up with more wealth and assets than most of their contributors. The irony is that members of their congregations worship a Christ whose lifestyle is in direct contrast with their own. Christ had nothing and owned nothing. He was entirely dependent on handouts. He was a vagabond comparable in status to the modern-day welfare recipient.

Random Thoughts from the Cosmos

"I don't really understand how you could have done this to me!"

[My response]
"Because it was so much fun."

Random Thoughts from the Cosmos

Some philosophers get into trouble when their search for truth ends up denying reality and even their own existence.

Random Thoughts from the Cosmos

Our choices are based somewhat on how desperate we are and what's available at the time.

Random Thoughts from the Cosmos

Some people advocate the return to the gold standard. In order for the U.S.A. to return to the gold standard, it would be necessary to establish a fixed price for gold — so many dollars for each ounce. One of the major stumbling blocks, unlike fifty years ago when it was illegal to possess gold, was it had to be sold to the government. Gold is now a commodity that is fair traded on an open market making it almost impossible to use as a base for printing money. For years the U.S.A. dollar has replaced gold as an international medium of exchange in the world marketplace even though it has no intrinsic value and is funded by debt.

Random Thoughts from the Cosmos

How are you going to create wealth if you don't print money funded by debt? Especially when we are more of a consumer nation than a producing nation. If you don't believe me, look at the trade balances between us and the Japanese and some of the other nations in the world.

Random Thoughts from the Cosmos

*Don't become too eager for truth o' man
for once you know truth, you may well
become a slave to it.*

Random Thoughts from the Cosmos

Social retardation is even a more common problem in this country than mental retardation.

Random Thoughts from the Cosmos

An egotist is one who is absolutely convinced that what he doesn't know really isn't worth knowing.

Random Thoughts from the Cosmos

A superior educational system is one which teaches you not only what to think but how to think. Many of the courses you take in school are based upon your ability to memorize the answers.

Random Thoughts from the Cosmos

Earth is a living hell when everything pleasurable is deemed to be evil or sinful.

Random Thoughts from the Cosmos

Happiness is believing that all of your faults and shortcomings are minor ones.

Random Thoughts from the Cosmos

Some of my closest friends have expressed a desire for a new experience. My suggestion was that they should try doing an honest day's work.

Random Thoughts from the Cosmos

Procrastination is the result of thinking those things which promise immediate rewards and happiness should have the highest priorities.

Random Thoughts from the Cosmos

Every new religion emerges during an era when established religions no longer fulfill the cultural needs of the people living in that locale or country.

Random Thoughts from the Cosmos

Truth somehow gets distorted by human emotions. Try to be objective about another man's beliefs and opinions whom you personally dislike or hate.

Random Thoughts from the Cosmos

Klint's Law

*Abstinence from one of life's little
pleasures generally leads to
overindulgence in others.*

Random Thoughts from the Cosmos

*Most people are hung up more on
propriety, titles, degrees, and
appearances than on knowledge, wisdom,
and common sense.*

Random Thoughts from the Cosmos

If a psychologist or a psychiatrist finds a pleasant, good-natured, and cooperative client who pays his or her fees regularly, the last thing he wants to do is to pronounce his patient cured or healed.

Random Thoughts from the Cosmos

If God has a body with a head, torso, and limbs who then made God? Something cannot be created out of nothing. The Creator, you see, is nothing more than the creation which can recreate itself.

Random Thoughts from the Cosmos

God stands tall in the pulpit every Sunday morning in every church in the land. Unfortunately, the only reference to a God-like man is the one delivering the sermon.

Random Thoughts from the Cosmos

What is the difference between a scholar and an intellectual? The scholar possesses the capability of memorizing the answers while the intellectual can think and reason things out for himself.

Random Thoughts from the Cosmos

The Bible tells you to love everyone, even your enemies. Now why would God tell you to do something that He, Himself would not do? Condemning a man to Hell is hardly a loving gesture.

Random Thoughts from the Cosmos

And let it be known amongst men that no man is ever condemned to eternal damnation. After all God has been portrayed, upon different occasions, as a God of love, charity, compassion, and understanding and not a God of wrath. True, there are quite a number of different portraits of God in the Bible. God is portrayed as a God of love, a God of wrath, a God of compassion, a God of vengeance, a God of obedience, a God of mercy, a God of Judgment, and a God of Justice. Pick whichever ones fit your particular philosophy of life and will allow you to live pretty much any life style you chose according to your own needs and desires.

Random Thoughts from the Cosmos

A builder is no less a god than the designer, draftsman, or architect. The total collective consciousness and knowledge of all beings past, present, and future are equivalent to the total creative capacity of God.

Random Thoughts from the Cosmos

Games begin when we assume there are universal truths which are binding on every human being. Most souls, who now find themselves in a body, migrated here from other dimensions, planes, and even other planets. We are not all bound by the same spiritual rules or laws. Some have had past lives here on earth. Others are entering this plane to learn lessons which they can only learn as an earthling and to experience certain pleasures not found anywhere else. Organized religion is just one of the necessary steps to achieving enlightenment in the evolution of the soul. Sometimes it appears, however, we are backsliding, but that is part of the evolutionary process.

Random Thoughts from the Cosmos

Rules, laws, and regulations were never made for me. They were made for the other guy who doesn't quite fit into a conventional pattern of behavior. You can always get around the law if you are important or wealthy enough. Why waste your time on me? Let's go after the real criminals. You know who I mean, those who rob convenient stores, use dope, drink alcohol, smoke marijuana, and violate juvenile curfew laws. These are the real criminals. Most white collar criminals, who have stolen millions, are really very likable and highly respected citizens. They are no-threat to society. So they made a mistake. Supposedly they are better candidates for rehabilitation.

Random Thoughts from the Cosmos

What are the negative aspects of positive thinking? Sooner or later you have to quit daydreaming of fame and fortune, get off your duff, and get back to work.

Random Thoughts from the Cosmos

*Many unhappy people dismiss sincere
and honest praise as flattery. They reject
it on the basis they deem themselves
unworthy. Maybe others can see some
good in them even though they cannot
see it in themselves.*

Random Thoughts from the Cosmos

*I could tell it the way it really happened,
but I wouldn't want to bore you.*

Random Thoughts from the Cosmos

The trouble with winning the really big one too early in life is that you may start thinking you are invincible, become complacent, and are totally unprepared when some unexpected event arises which sends you to the bottomless pits of despair and gloom.

Random Thoughts from the Cosmos

There are three types of drinkers — the social drinker, the problem drinker, and those of us who like it.

Random Thoughts from the Cosmos

There is a big movement in this country to increase speed limits. We wear seat belts to protect lives and now we want to increase speed limits which will increase the number of accidents and deaths. If we raise the speed limits, will the cost in lives exceed those caused by secondary tobacco smoke? If the answer is, yes, then we should do away with the no smoking ban in public buildings and restaurants and let the speedsters go to it. No matter what the speed limits are, people still exceed them. If everybody abided by the speed limits, look how many lives we could save? If you received a speeding ticket lately, you would probably like to see all speed limits eliminated. Don't we want to make this country safe for everyone not just for nonsmokers? Oh I see! You want others to make certain concessions but not you.

Random Thoughts from the Cosmos

A candidate for political office frequently makes promises that the other party and even members of his own party won't allow him to keep, even if he does get elected. Then comes along a president or a governor, which in all probability you didn't vote for, and vetoes the bill that your elected official promised you he would defend or pass. Furthermore, most politicians promise so much that the public soon forgets what it was the politicians promised in the first place.

Random Thoughts from the Cosmos

Since God is said to be all knowing and all powerful, and since man was created in His image, it is little wonder why man tries to imitate Him. Most men make an effort to think, act, and behave as if they were the Creator. Those Christians, who are the vanguards of morality and decency, will soon be enmeshed in a morass of legalities as to what the rules and penalties should be for violating the moral code and to what extent the government should have in enforcing them. This may cause such widespread dissension that the police and U.S.A. troops will be ordered to kill on sight those protesters and demonstrators opposed to government involvement. Tobacco, drugs, and alcohol are but the major forerunners to a highly volatile and controlled society. Hitler discovered that the best way to control people was to take away all their moral prerogatives and impose the death penalty upon those who don't conform. There was no trial by a jury. Yes, it can happen here with the assistance of the Moral Majority.

Random Thoughts from the Cosmos

Life has its delays and detours. Don't curse the situation. Relax and look around. You may see something you would not have otherwise seen or learn something you would not have otherwise known. Learn to capitalize on every adversity.

Random Thoughts from the Cosmos

You are loved if you think you are. You are unloved if you think you are. But what do our thoughts about things have to do with reality anyway? Maybe we are and maybe we aren't, and most of us will never know for sure.

Random Thoughts from the Cosmos

When people think they are thinking, in all probability, all they are doing is reacting in some automatic, spontaneous, and almost predictable manner. It all depends what has been previously fed into the mind's computer and how you have been programmed as to how you are going to think and respond.

Random Thoughts from the Cosmos

*Every goal is made up of a series of
smaller goals. Each smaller goal is made
up of details. If you don't enjoy doing
the details, you will find little joy and
happiness in achieving your goal. But if
you achieved your goal, but had no fun
or happiness in achieving it, you will
have deprived yourself of one of life's
most gratifying experiences.*

Random Thoughts from the Cosmos

Let it be known that sex is not only for procreation but a means by which you can achieve a psychological release from frustrations, anxieties, and the pressures of daily living. Be cautious o' man, for anything which can give great pleasure can also cause great harm.

Random Thoughts from the Cosmos

If you get bored and feel trapped, then perhaps you may have to risk something — your security, your life, your health, your wealth, your marriage, or your reputation. Fear may dominate and control your life. It is better to have gambled and lost than to live the rest of your life with regrets.

Random Thoughts from the Cosmos

*When God answers his followers'
prayers, it seems the recipients are
always around to remind us that we too
could be on a winning team. When their
prayers go unanswered, we are told that
it was not God's will, for He knows
what's best for us. Some say their
prayers are denied because He is testing
them to see if they are truly committed.
Under those circumstances, how would
you ever know for sure, if He was even
listening or the least bit concerned?*

Random Thoughts from the Cosmos

Our likes and dislikes, loves and hates,
prejudices, and behavior are conditioned
as much by the people we dislike or hate
as by those we like and love. The
subtleties as to why we prefer one thing
or person over another are all part of a
highly complex series of actions and
reactions which are no longer discernible
to human consciousness, which imposes
certain limitations on our free will. In
fact, they could render us a helpless
victim to our fate.

Random Thoughts from the Cosmos

If I were to solve all of my problems, I would have to go out and create some new ones so I will have something to converse upon. After all, what is there to talk about anyway? It is a problem oriented world, and if you don't believe me, just pick up the daily newspaper and read it.

Random Thoughts from the Cosmos

People have expressed an interest and desire in changing some aspects of their character. Before you can be reprogrammed, however, you have to be deprogrammed, which means giving up old and meaningless habits, changing some of your attitudes, and ridding yourself of a lot of erroneous beliefs and superstitions.

Random Thoughts from the Cosmos

*Are people more important than things?
You can control yourself and things
easier than other people. The respect
which you should seek the most is that
associated with knowledge, talents, and
abilities rather than resorting to
deception or manipulation.*

Random Thoughts from the Cosmos

Perhaps even erroneous beliefs are better than none at all provided they are not being challenged by those who wish to impose their own beliefs upon us. Our beliefs can cause great stress and anxiety when they are unacceptable to one's children, brothers, sisters, parents and relatives. Beliefs can cause as many psychological problems and hard feelings as those which arise from arguments, physical abuse, temper, and undesirable personal habits.

Random Thoughts from the Cosmos

If you blame your parents and environment for all of your misfortunes in life, perhaps, your parents' only defense is to blame their parents. This, according to Bible, goes all the way back to the Garden of Eden when the first man and woman partook of the fruit from the tree of knowledge at the persistent beckoning of that lowly snake. Supposedly what happened thousands of years ago has had an affect on man's free will ever since. He has been waging an uphill struggle with temptation from the beginning of humanity. Why should I be punished for the sins of Adam and Eve? That's not fair. This is a formal protest.

Random Thoughts from the Cosmos

Evidently alcohol has some redeeming value or why would people use it? When taken in moderation it can be stimulating, uplifting, and physically relaxing. Alcohol brings out the best in some and the worst in others, but that's true of almost everything. Even religion makes some people belligerent and wanting to kill. Religion sanctions wars fought between nations of different faiths. Even though the Bible says "thou shalt not kill," some Christians believe in capital punishment, killing homosexuals, using guns in self-defense, fighting wars, exceeding the speed limit, and murdering abortion doctors. Alcohol and tobacco may be responsible for a few deaths, but that's next to nothing compared to the number of innocent people killed by guns. Do away with guns then arguments against alcohol and tobacco may be heard.

Random Thoughts from the Cosmos

It helps if you tell God off from time to time. He needs to know that you are unhappy with the present administration, and that you believe in equal time, rights, and privileges.

He may not hear you, but at least you've unloaded your burden on someone who can't hurt you. If He can't hear you, He won't hurt you.

Random Thoughts from the Cosmos

The purpose of tithing back in the days of Abraham was to set aside 10% of the annual crop for the years when droughts or disasters laid the land unproductive. Now the clergy use their tithes and offerings not for the poor and needy but for salaries and vain monuments of glass, steel, and stone as memorials to some man's ego who affirms that only Christians are entitled to reside in paradise.

Random Thoughts from the Cosmos

If psychiatrists and psychologists spent as much time trying to figure out why happy people are happy as they do trying to find the causes for neurosis, psychosis and unhappiness, they would probably make a valuable contribution to this society. They will probably never know since no one is ever going to pay such exorbitant fees for the privilege of telling their counselors why they are happy.

Random Thoughts from the Cosmos

*Man is part animal, and he needs
stroking as much as animals do. People
need:*
patting
cuddling
hugging
sexual intercourse
touching
massaging
embracing
kissing
*These are forms of nonverbal
communication which express mutual
approval and love for others.*

Random Thoughts from the Cosmos

Birth is a miracle. The human body is a miracle. All man-made products and objects are miracles. All intelligence and man's great fund of knowledge is a miracle. All crafts, skills, and talents are miracles. All of creation is a miracle. Marvel at this universe and behold the great variety and intricacy in nature and science. Everything is a miracle no matter how simple or complex.

Random Thoughts from the Cosmos

The sex drive and needs vary greatly from person to person. However, if you are unattractive, have a personality deficiency, or have a handicap, you might be highly grateful for sex-related novels, massage parlors, and pornography. Sex may be available to some men and women whenever they need or desire it; but for those less fortunate, they must sublimate their desires by relating to a world of sexual fantasies. Pornography, contrary to public belief, reduces the incidence of rape according to studies conducted in Denmark.

Random Thoughts from the Cosmos

Every human is a magnet. He attracts others unto himself who are vital to his development and evolution. Some say its chemistry. Others say it's vibrations. But whether it is chemistry or vibrations, it involves mathematical formulas and geometric patterns. What are called coincidences are attractions by symbols, numbers, colors, names, locations, sounds, and definitions, which explains our affinity or repulsion for those who are drawn into our spheres of influence.

Random Thoughts from the Cosmos

Two men confronted with danger of losing their lives each prayed to God that he might return home safely after an airplane crash. Their friends, family, and relatives did likewise, but tragically, one of the two died. The other lived to give testimonials as to how his faith had sustained and saved him but then died of a lingering illness (cancer) five years later. The irony of this situation is the one who died first made it to heaven just that much sooner and was rewarded for being such a devout Christian. If the afterlife is such a great and glorious experience, why should we grieve over the ones who have made their transition? We should be happy for them.

Random Thoughts from the Cosmos

Some say that morality should be based upon the concept that anything is right, moral, and ethical as long as it doesn't hurt anyone else. The only problem is that self interests are generally in opposition to what may be in the best interest of the public as a whole. Those who do nothing to try to improve society seem to antagonize others by the fact that they abstain from doing something. Anyone who says you can live in this world without hurting someone is living under an illusion simply because people attach different motives to what one does and says and will impute their own feelings and emotions onto any given situation.

Random Thoughts from the Cosmos

Is there any factual or circumstantial evidence that man has a soul? In other words is there any proof that the mind (soul) has a separate and independent existence aside from that of the body? There are philosophers who believe that the mind and soul are inextricably one and the same. We know that the mind does not register pain when the body is given an appropriate anesthetic. But how do you explain why the mind fails to register pain when a person is in a deeply mesmerized state induced by a hypnotist? Surgery has been performed without using drugs — only hypnosis.

Random Thoughts from the Cosmos

Is God an anthropomorphic being or a creative principle? Is there a Supreme Being who rules the universe single handed or are there any number of beings who form a celestial hierarchy and influence mortal thought and intelligence? Could it be that these beings exist in dimensions that vibrate at such high frequencies that they are invisible and undetectable to all those except those who possess extra-sensory perception?

Random Thoughts from the Cosmos

Many Christian denominations provide an escape clause just in case you can't live up to the high moral standards that are expected from their members. The clergy have led many to believe that "once you're saved you're always saved." This type of religious philosophy is not always conducive to striving for moral and ethical excellence but encourages the type of behavior it is trying to prevent. It makes hypocrites out of people, for you are stating, in essence, that you can bend or brake the laws of God at will, and you will not be held accountable for them on judgment day.

Random Thoughts from the Cosmos

Heaven is a place where your fantasies become realities. As your life begins to unfold, you may slowly start to learn that your heaven, however, is right here on earth. For others, and possibly yourself as well, this life is hell, and thus you are now looking forward to taking up a permanent residence in the promised land.

Random Thoughts from the Cosmos

The Politician's Motto

"I'll vote for your bill if you'll vote for mine."

Random Thoughts from the Cosmos

It's not what you say that is wrong, it's your presentation.

Random Thoughts from the Cosmos

The one who rejects you is generally the one you love most of all.

Random Thoughts from the Cosmos

Most things deemed good, when done in excess, become evil or bad.

Random Thoughts from the Cosmos

To conquer adversity requires you to make some changes in your personality, habits, beliefs, opinions, or attitude.

Random Thoughts from the Cosmos

The one thing that ecologists have failed to find a solution for is mind pollutants. You know what I mean — that propaganda that teachers, ministers, priests, and politicians try to make us believe is unequivocally or universally true. Even scientists have some reservation about absolutes.

Random Thoughts from the Cosmos

Apparently not all Christian countries in this world hold the view that nudity is a form of pornography. In Scandinavia, you will find nude statues and nude beaches as part of their culture. The human body is an acceptable art form in northern Europe. Due to the puritan influence imprinted on the U.S.A. from colonial days, we are determined to create a world where everything pleasurable is deemed to be sinful. The large contingencies of Christian-right and Fundamentalist evangelists have discovered there is a direct relationship between the amount of time devoted to preaching about sin and the amount of money garnered for the church coffers.

Random Thoughts from the Cosmos

Any publicly involving a political sex scandal hurts a politician's credibility as an efficient administrator more than if he were known to be a liar, cheat, or raider upon the public treasuries.

Random Thoughts from the Cosmos

Adam and Eve were the first man and woman, and they had but three children Abel, Cain, and Seth — all boys. So where did they find their wives? Could it be one or all three of Eve's sons had sex with their mother only to marry their sisters? Who performed the marriage ceremony? Or did they just live with one another in sin?

Random Thoughts from the Cosmos

Ecclesiastes Chapter 3:1-3.4 To everything there is a season, and a time to every purpose under the heaven, a time to be born, and a time to die; a time to plant, and a time to pluck up that which is planted; a time to kill, and a time to heal; a time to break down, and a time to build up; a time to weep, and a time to laugh; a time to mourn, and a time to dance; 3.7-3.8 a time to reap, and a time to sew; a time to keep silence, and a time to speak; a time to love, and a time to hate; a time of war, and a time of peace.

Several questions arise from reading these scriptures: First, these verses seem to have a tinge of fatalism written into them as if every event in our lives is arranged according to some universal time table. Second, it appears that killing, war, and hate are part of the eternal scheme of things offering little hope for an enduring peace. If everything is predetermined, how can man be held accountable for his sins?

Random Thoughts from the Cosmos

*The Bible is an antiquated book that no longer
fills the social or cultural needs of our society.
The Bible is supposed to be a book of prophecy
and yet it does not contain a vernacular of words
meaningful to the 20th and 21st centuries.
There are millions of words in the Bible, but the
following words cannot be found in the King
James Version.*

- alcohol • tobacco • drugs • pornography
- homosexual • lesbian • incest • smoking
- rape • sex • sexist • women's lib • intercourse
- gay • abortion • masturbation • Communism
- Socialism • Democracy • destiny • greed
- gangs • white race • discrimination • bigotry
- racist • racism • guns • jury • nuclear
- selfish • juvenile delinquency • media
- adolescence • stress • anxiety • frustration
- freeways • radio • telecommunications • clones
- TV • telephone • space capsules • UFOs
- newspapers • automobiles • free enterprise
- airplanes • pyramids • capitalism • cameras
- United States • Russia • China • cave man
- civil rights • environment • pollution • Bible
- night clubs • taverns • toilets • men's room
- women's room • restrooms • defecate
- urinate • bath tubs • showers • kitchens
- vegetables • sports • entertainment • hobby

Random Thoughts from the Cosmos

• *internal combustion* • *playing cards* • *bingo*
• *competition* • *ethics* • *morals* • *scruples*
• *pregnant* • *hospital* • *medical doctor* • *football*
• *baseball* • *basketball* • *gymnastics*
• *child abuse* • *spousal abuse* • *dictionary*
• *atheist* • *agnostic* • *libraries*

And many other words too numerous to mention. One of the reasons we don't update the Bible is because we derive so much pleasure in trying to interpret it. It seems that by leaving it in some archaic dialect, we all get to spend endless hours trying to figure out the gist of what it is trying to say. Do you understand Shakespearean English? Remember the King James Bible was written in the same era as Shakespeare.

Random Thoughts from the Cosmos

In the very first sentence of Genesis 1:1 of the Bible, it states: "In the beginning God created the heaven and the earth." Now the question is: "What does the word heaven mean?" When I look up in the sky on a clear night, I refer to the stars as the heavens and not the heaven. Or are we referring to that place where the souls of Christians migrate upon their demise from earth? Why would God create a heaven before he had a need for one? Who do you suppose the first Christians ever to enter heaven were? Surely their names would have been worthy of mention in the Bible. If there is such a thing as a beginning, then there must be a first of everything. Remember no one goes to heaven who isn't a Christian. So some man or woman had to be heaven's first arrival. Everyone who lived prior to the first-saved Christian must have gone to hell or reincarnated in purgatory as another human being. Time never stops long enough to make a finite line between a beginning and an ending.

Random Thoughts from the Cosmos

Due to the influence of the Christian Coalition and conservative-right-wing Christianity, more and more laws are being passed every day to prevent juveniles from experimenting with life. No cigarettes, no alcohol, no sex, no drugs, no pornography, no loitering, no driving up and down main street on weekend nights, no "R" or "X" rated movies, no sex and violence on television, no place to go after school, no roller-blading, no computer "internet", no "sexy" sitcoms, no profanity, no access to nude magazines, and no criticism of adults.

Suggestion: Allow children to do whatever their parents do as long as they do not interfere with the lifestyles of other kids. This is known as "family values."

Random Thoughts from the Cosmos

Instead of trying to figure out the causes as to why our jails and prisons are overcrowded with young adults, we would rather spend more money in building prisons and jails to house them than to look at the psychological and sociological roots behind their deviant behavior. Probably, the truth of the matter is that we are not interested in the causes behind teenage crime, for it would require that we would have to have an indepth study of ourselves and the society we live in. And that analysis would have to include the church's role as being a willing and responsible participant in setting the tempo for increased violence. As soon as we, including the church's demand for moral conformity, pass more laws to prohibit certain types of behavior, the perception is: there will be less crime and discension. Many feel that as soon as we do away with the welfare system the less crime we will have. Most Americans would rather pay $25,000 to $35,000 a year to house a prisoner in jail than give it to him and his family to live on. That is only part of the cost. While a person is in jail, we may have to pay welfare to his family to live on.

Random Thoughts from the Cosmos

There are many Christian countries throughout the world which permit public nude beaches and pools. That's not true in the U.S.A. where nude is considered lewd. Many of the paintings of God show him naked. Perhaps we should commission some artists to paint a shirt and a pair of pants to cover all His private parts. We should remove all the naked statues of God and put them in storage until a more liberal generation is voted into office. God forbid that any young woman or girl should ever see a penis anytime prior to her wedding night.

Random Thoughts from the Cosmos

Accurate statistics are hard to come by as we have little or no knowledge as to how statistics are gathered. Only the federal government has the capability of keeping tabs on what is transpiring here in the U.S., but as to who decides on what statistical data is to be kept, how the data is to be collected, and who can dispense it, no one probably knows since it all is part of a gigantic bureaucracy. No one challenges the government on its statistics. Few if any, has any understanding as to how the Department of Statistics operates. When information is requested by another agency to the Department of Statistics, then the requested information must be returned to the agency making the request. There is probably not one single person who can trace how and where the government got its information relative to the relationship between secondary tobacco smoke and lung cancer. If the head of the EPA or the Surgeon General makes a statement on the effects of secondary tobacco smoke who on his staff of subordinates would dare challenge a superior's proclamation but what they would be putting their job in jeopardy. Whoever heads a federal agency is free to make any statement he likes whether it is an honest statement of fact or not.

Random Thoughts from the Cosmos

Happiness is knowing which one is going to be one too many.

Random Thoughts from the Cosmos

If you interpret the Bible literally, how can you interpret the phrase "to be born again" to mean anything but reincarnation?

Random Thoughts from the Cosmos

Truth changes with the acquisition of new knowledge, which means it is changing daily. This is true not only for science but religion as well.

Random Thoughts from the Cosmos

*To be a winner, you can't change your
mind every day or two.*

Don't underestimate the power of those who think just as positively as you do and who have aspirations to eliminate you as a competitor.

Random Thoughts from the Cosmos

Everybody is born to the parents he is supposed to have. Everybody lives in the time frame he is supposed to live in. Everybody is at the place he is supposed to be. Everybody is doing what he is supposed to do. Everyone is on an evolutionary-time trip. Everyone who's judgmental cannot help being judgmental. You have to love and accept everybody for what they are. These are the concepts of one who believes in predestination. To believe otherwise means you are the center of the universe and that you manipulate and control everything that transpires around you. If you think you are a spokesperson for God, then you must be God.

Random Thoughts from the Cosmos

One main criticism received from reviewers of this book is the amount of time and space given to alcohol, tobacco, drugs, prostitution, sex, gambling, firearms, and pornography. Considerable space has been used in this book questioning the wisdom as to whether moral and ethical issues should be subjected to legislative and legal control and should the violators be subject to criminal prosecution. Could the so-called cure be worse than the disease? Living in a police state will not be fun, and when legislators can't find anything else to do, they will try to find another freedom to take away from us just in order to keep busy. Of course, nobody wants to do away with Las Vegas and sin city. We all need a refuge from time to time where we can go and be somebody other than ourselves.

Random Thoughts from the Cosmos

It is easier to ask a total stranger a personal question than to ask an acquaintance. It is rather interesting what total strangers are willing to divulge about themselves, especially, when it is highly unlikely you have any common friends. Don't be afraid to ask questions and then listen attentively and carefully. It is surprising sometimes what you may learn if you're not afraid to ask questions even if they are the highly-personal type. Most of us are interested, to some degree, in exploiting others either for knowledge or profit. A stranger may prove to be a valuable contact.

Random Thoughts from the Cosmos

If each man has free will then God has lost control of his universe.

Random Thoughts from the Cosmos

*There are two ways of doing something,
my dear — your way and the right way.*

Random Thoughts from the Cosmos

The question is not whether one should get involved. The question is how does one get uninvolved should one choose to do so.

Random Thoughts from the Cosmos

If you were able to get even one small glimpse of truth once in your lifetime, it would be a rare but rewarding experience.

Random Thoughts from the Cosmos

You are programmed as much by your enemies as you are by your friends.

Random Thoughts from the Cosmos

Before burning all your bridges behind you, be sure you know how to swim. You might wish to make a hasty retreat.

Random Thoughts from the Cosmos

If you haven't had any new thoughts in years, tune into the Cosmic hot line. To tune in you have to get focused. It's called the ancient art of Zen meditation.

Random Thoughts from the Cosmos

A Prophecy

At a time when the country is enjoying its greatest period of prosperity, along comes a political party with a political novice and hack as its leader who convinces the electorate — not by facts and figures — but by rhetoric that unless we radically change the system we are going to be in serious trouble. Once the budget is slashed dramatically and the system drastically reduced to a mere pittance of what it was, it will cause massive layoffs and unemployment amongst its citizenry with no hope of ever getting any welfare benefits following in the wake of one of the greatest depressions ever to hit the United States.

Random Thoughts from the Cosmos

Did God ever envision the day when He might create someone greater than Himself? What was it that Jesus promised? Book of John, Chapter 14, verse 12: "Verily, verily, I say unto you. He that believeth in me, the works that I do, shall he do also; and greater works than these shall he do because I go unto the Father." Followed by verses 13 and 14. "And whatsoever ye shall ask in my name that will I do that the Father may be glorified in heaven. If ye shall ask anything in my name I will do it."

So why not pray to be God? It might be fun to be God for a while. I'm sure I couldn't do any worse managing the affairs of the earth than the God we now have.

Random Thoughts from the Cosmos

About the time you have everything figured out, someone comes along and plants a seed of reasonable doubt.

Random Thoughts from the Cosmos

The only reason this world turns is because it is caught up in a vortex created by love and hate.

Random Thoughts from the Cosmos

If I have to die, may it be to atone for
the sins of those self-righteous,
politically-oriented, fundamentalist,
right-winged, Conservative,
Fundamentalist Christians who believe
that "family values" should coincide
with "church values." It wouldn't be
such a tragedy if the Bible could be
authenticated by some type of proof. If
you are interested in trying to prove the
validity of the Bible, you could start by
learning "Aramaic." For you to prove
that the Bible is infallible, you would
have to prove that the people who did the
translation for the King James Version
of the Bible were also infallible.

Random Thoughts from the Cosmos

Truth is not for the faint hearted! It will destroy most of your preconceived ideas about what it is.

Random Thoughts from the Cosmos

If reason is your stock and trade, you'll starve to death. Your basic appeal should be to the emotions.

Random Thoughts from the Cosmos

Happiness is taking half truths and convincing others that they are gospel truths.

Random Thoughts from the Cosmos

Should violations of the moral and ethical code be handled by parents or the police? Morality is now legislated, and it now looks as if we are headed toward becoming a "police state." Families will have very little to say about how their children will be raised. The schools, churches, and the government will be assuming greater roles in the indoctrination and teaching of our children as to what is morally proper. The government will pass laws to reinforce those teachings and let the police rather than the parents do the disciplining. The children will then be taught to be informers as to who is breaking the law. Perhaps one can better understand why couples prefer to live with one another rather than getting married, and why women want abortions rather than having children.

Random Thoughts from the Cosmos

*The whole world is on the move. Most of
its populous has only a vague
recollection of where they've been and
very little idea of where they're going.*

Random Thoughts from the Cosmos

If you have a sense of humor and don't take yourself too seriously, there is very little likelihood you will ever have to be institutionalized.

Random Thoughts from the Cosmos

Statistics are frequently used to prove whatever statisticians want them to prove. These are the tools of a manipulator to inflame human emotions. Why should the government want to control your thoughts? Why do they want to make a mountain out of a mole hill? It is just one of many small steps necessary in its efforts to gain total dominion over each and every one of its citizens. After all, a dictatorship is the most efficient means of running a government. If you don't believe me, visit China, Iran, Iraq, or Saudia Arabia. It's fun to protest but not at the expense of becoming a political prisoner.

A Morning Prayer

Dear Lord, if you can't use me constructively, at least make me a good obstacle. Why waste a perfectly good day?

Random Thoughts from the Cosmos

Before anyone can react to you in any way other than the way they have previously, you will have to act, behave, and react differently than you have in the past.

Random Thoughts from the Cosmos

Reality is greatly distorted by your sensory impressions, prejudices, biases, emotions, desires, and what you have been trained and educated to observe.

Random Thoughts from the Cosmos

The rape of the human mind is far more likely than that of the body. Someone is always trying to put something into one's head which it wants to consciously resist and reject.

Random Thoughts from the Cosmos

I have tried, upon occasion, to figure out what Jesus might say, if he were alive today to this question: "Should someone murder a loved one or accidentally kill him or her while driving drunk, should I love the perpetrator or hate him?" The answer may be found in the Bible, and throughout the scriptures there is great emphasis on love and forgiveness. One life has already been taken. Shall we destroy another out of retribution and bitterness? Nothing good ever comes from hate. Treat the criminal as if he were one of your own.

From Mark 12:31: "Thou shalt love thy neighbor as thyself." From Luke 6:37 "Judge ye not, and ye shall not be judged: condemn not, and ye shall not be condemned: Forgive, and ye shall be forgiven."

Why don't Christians read their Bibles?

Random Thoughts from the Cosmos

Most of us have given some thought on how we can make ourselves desirable. Many of us would first have to lose some weight, but then we would have to do something about our personality and behavior. Maybe we should just give up and accept ourselves the way we are. It's not impossible to lose weight, but I wonder about this personality and behavior modification bit.

Random Thoughts from the Cosmos

I could better cope with life if I didn't have someone constantly reminding me that I should have a conscience. Someday me and that conscience are going to have a permanent parting of the ways.

Random Thoughts from the Cosmos

Can't help but wonder if they tell jokes abroad about the stupid Americans just as we tell Polish jokes. After all, how many other countries throughout this world send foreign aid to their enemies?

Random Thoughts from the Cosmos

Politicians pass laws which do nothing
but redistribute the power and wealth
amongst its citizenry. They take money,
rights, and privileges away from
some — usually from the poor and
middle class — and give it to those who
least need it.

Random Thoughts from the Cosmos

Conflict will always be part of the ever changing scenes of time. It will be with us as long as man is endowed with an imagination and is dissatisfied with his present lot in life.

Random Thoughts from the Cosmos

*Every ending always precipitates a new
beginning. Every effect becomes a new
cause. Death is not only an ending but a
new beginning. Death is but birth in
another dimension.*

Random Thoughts from the Cosmos

Anyone who states that he will not play anyone else's games will find it difficult to enlist the support and cooperation of others in helping him to play his game.

Random Thoughts from the Cosmos

Is it better to be a happy slave than an unhappy master? Remember, the more freedom you have, the more responsibility you have. Perhaps freedom is an illusion.

Religion could not survive on Christ's affirmations on "love" alone. Evidently without fear and guilt the church would have no power or control over the minds of mankind, and thus the church would not survive. Then to guarantee the survival of the church, the ministry has to assure their flocks that heaven is at hand for those who abide by the teachings in the scriptures. Seekers of truth, however, will have to go beyond the perimeters of the Bible and pursue an independent course of study. Religion is for the masses. Truth is almost an endless pursuit — at least in this lifetime.

Random Thoughts from the Cosmos

Some people are so busy planning and organizing their work, they find little or no time to perform.

Random Thoughts from the Cosmos

*Do it unto others before they have a
chance to do it unto you and you become
a self-proclaimed winner. The
consequences, however, may be
devastating. Wounded egos frequently
seek ways to retaliate.*

Random Thoughts from the Cosmos

You can't put positive thoughts into a
garbage container. Sooner or later you
have to do an in-depth analysis of the
negative self. A positive input can be
negated by erroneous beliefs, guilt, fear,
false information, and making
premature judgments.

Random Thoughts from the Cosmos

To give unselfishly and excessively is to say another person's needs are more important than your own. Man needs to retain a balanced program of action. Excesses of all kinds lead to severe and devastating problems. You should know by now, you can't have it your way all the time — you may have to compromise your position from time to time even if you have a strong will to do otherwise.

Random Thoughts from the Cosmos

How would you know paradise unless you could contrast it with something else? Knowledge of good and evil is nothing more than a study of contrasts. There would be no "evil" unless you can define "good." For instance, there could be no beginning without an ending. The Bible is in error to say "in the beginning" — meaning you're starting at point zero. Sorry, you cannot create something out of nothing unless it is, of course, a fantasy, but then there is always something happening that zaps you back to reality.

Random Thoughts from the Cosmos

Some people manipulate and control others through fear or by trying to make them feel guilty about some of the things they've done. Others accomplish much more through love and kindness without the backlash of resentment and hate.

Random Thoughts from the Cosmos

The best man does not always get the recognition he deserves. He isn't very smart if he is convinced that he doesn't need a good public relations agent and that games aren't necessary to maximize his potential.

Random Thoughts from the Cosmos

Perhaps the happiest people are the conformists who are aware of the boundaries beyond which they dare not cross, but who learn to find ways to derive the maximum pleasure, freedom, and creativity within the perimeters of their own social, political, and economic confines.

Random Thoughts from the Cosmos

Unhappy people are attracted to and by other unhappy people. A winner doesn't care to associate with losers any longer than necessary, unless, of course, he can figure out a way that he can exploit something from a relationship for personal gain. For the most part, we attract what we are, but all of that can change — sometimes merely by moving to a new locale or community where we can take on a new identity and make some new friends.

Random Thoughts from the Cosmos

It's hard to believe, but there are people who don't want to know what's going on in this world. For once they are aware, they might feel obligated to try to resolve some of its problems. Besides, you can't be held responsible if you don't listen to the news or read the newspaper and are unaware as to what's transpiring globally or locally. "Let someone else worry about those big problems. I have enough of my own. Who cares about what goes on in the halls of congress? Why concern myself about the issues or political reform? There may be better ways of running the government, but I say, look out for number one first. Starving kids and inadequate medical care is none of my concern."

Random Thoughts from the Cosmos

And who amongst you who calls himself an atheist, agnostic, or believer can accept or deny the existence of God when you have no unanimous agreement as to whom or what God is in the first place. How can you argue over the existence of a Being which can't be defined? The only question worth speculating upon is: "Does man have a soul which survives death?" What evidence do we have that man is immortal? Is there any circumstantial evidence to support such a claim? Have you ever been hypnotized and regressed to a previous lifetime?

Random Thoughts from the Cosmos

If Christ were to incarnate today and observe the antics of most Christians, he would shake his head in disbelief. How could they take the simple message of love and distort and pervert it to such a degree that it has become the breeding ground for hate, prejudice, and bigotry?

Random Thoughts from the Cosmos

Would there be a world had you never been born? The world only exists because you have a conscious awareness of it. If this is true, will there be a world after you die? Some philosophers find the answers to these questions as a basis for their belief that the human soul is immortal and indestructible.

Random Thoughts from the Cosmos

If you were happy and contented before
you became wealthy or successful,
chances are things aren't going to
change too much. But if you were
unhappy and discontented when you had
little if any assets, no amount of money
is going to change your disposition or
your general outlook on life.

Random Thoughts from the Cosmos

I will vote for the first politician who will promise to sponsor a bill prohibiting any further legislation or who will repeal many of the laws already on the books. Whoever heard of a law being repealed? We have passed so many laws it takes a lawyer to find a law that predates an earlier law which contradicts the intent of the newest one. Most of the legislation being passed today has to do with restraints on morality. Our freedom to let families make choices is slowly disappearing. We are perfectly content to let some religion, church, or coalition make our choices and decisions for us.

Random Thoughts from the Cosmos

Now the question arises, "If man could create life, would man then be God to the thing he created?" The ministry and the clergy have taken the position that creating life was the one thing God could do that man could never do. Have you been reading the latest scientific journals? We can now split a cell and create two of something when nature (God) intended there be only one. It is called cloning.

Random Thoughts from the Cosmos

As long as everything is going well for us, we have that sense of omnipotence and being the captain of our ship. But don't forget about the pirates and the unforeseen contingencies of weather while you are feeling complacent. The only time you question your infallibility is when you begin to feel that gravitational pull of being sucked into someone else's orbit and are being manipulated in the process.

Random Thoughts from the Cosmos

*How can you make an acceptable moral
or ethical choice when you have detected
some basic flaws and contradictions in
the scriptures? No man should be
obligated to accept any belief that is
predicated strictly on faith. The logical
man's choice will be determined by
assessing his chances in terms of reward
and punishment rather than on
controversial religious teachings, which
are based upon hundreds of different
interpretations from any number of
different translations. No one really
knows for sure which language Christ
spoke. I doubt seriously if it was
English.*

Random Thoughts from the Cosmos

Politicians have been promising us a cure-all for the ills of this society ever since we became a country. Now even if they could put their cure-alls in a pill or a small capsule, I am certain, someone would be allergic to it. Some people claim that the answers lie in drugs, which may not solve the problems of our society, but it may help us to take flight from reality occasionally until things are finally resolved.

Random Thoughts from the Cosmos

At what point in time and space does an egg cease to be an egg and becomes an embryo for a new creation? What infused it with life at that split second? What activates the creative process? Is the process totally an internal one or is their some mysterious ray from a cosmic source that sparks the creative development of the embryo?

Random Thoughts from the Cosmos

An addiction is any substance, activity, or compulsion from which you derive pleasure or which lessens pain or the avoidance of pain and is performed or taken at frequent intervals. To abstain from such a substance, activity, or compulsion would cause anxiety, loss of continuity, inability to concentrate, or great discomfort. Most addictions are never overcome until they become a health hazard or start interfering with one's job, social standing, security, family harmony, running afoul of the law or until a more desirable addiction can be found as a substitute. Any activity whether it is substance abuse or a hobby, habit, religion, recreation, business, or job when done in excess is an addiction whenever it interferes with living a balanced and productive life. Most of our excesses are not considered immoral such as prescription drugs, gambling on lottery tickets, exceeding the

Random Thoughts from the Cosmos

speed limit, eating between meals, shopping and buying things we don't need, drinking alcoholic beverages, spending long hours watching television, working in excess of 40 hours a week, giving excessive amounts in time and money to the church, etc. Most addicts can cope very easily until their activity is deemed to be unlawful, causes an allergy or illness, or becomes a social stigma. The laws on smoking are unreasonable when you consider all the other addictions which have social approval but are far more dangerous. Not all addictions are illegal or immoral and those which are not, may be, nonetheless, harmful to the body causing serious illnesses, emotional instability, nervousness, and mental traumas; but these addictions are seldom the type that gets any media attention. Most addictions are multi-daily "fixes" such as drinking coffee at regular intervals during the day or drinking a can of soda now and then during the course of the working day (often as a substitute for tobacco). Many habits or addictions are not generally viewed from their long-term effects, but as a means of soothing the nerves or as a relaxant whenever one needs some immediate relief from stress or anxiety. Many smokers have quit the habit because they fear of being ostracized by other employees or customers. By the way, many of our allergies to tobacco could be caused by twenty years of negative conditioning by the Surgeon General, the EPA, and the AMA — all making claims about secondary tobacco smoke which can't be substantiated. Why did they do it? To create the belief that they are interested in your welfare when, in fact, those agencies aren't even the least bit interested in whether the average citizen even has any health insurance.

Random Thoughts from the Cosmos

*When you die and go to heaven, you
will be more than amply provided for.
There will be a reconciliation with
friends and relatives — no arguments, no
strife, no problems, no war, no need to
work. It might be all right for a short
but long overdue rest, but out of sheer
boredom, you might decide to
reincarnate to seek the varieties that
only a planet like Earth has to offer.*

Random Thoughts from the Cosmos

The Bible does not go into any great detail as to why Satan got kicked out of heaven. So why did he? Some possible reasons are given below.

> (a) Because he got damn tired of being a "yes" man.
> (b) Because he was challenging God for His job.
> (c) Because he wanted to be a devil's advocate.
> (d) Because he got tired of the dictatorship.
> (e) Because he started developing the ability to think for himself.
> (f) Because he got bored for the lack of any challenges.
> (g) All of the above.

Random Thoughts from the Cosmos

Is man free? Is he predestined to be who he is? What is beautiful? What is meaningful? Who or what is God? What is of value or has value? What is good and what is evil? What is right and what is wrong? What is reality? Why does man suffer? What is man's responsibility to his fellow man? Some say truth is absolute. Others say truth should be based upon what makes one happy, comfortable, and conscience free.

Random Thoughts from the Cosmos

Some Christian denominations deem dancing to be sinful. Actually, dancing is mentally and physically therapeutic. Dancing has long been a traditional and integral part of religious ceremonies of primitive and ancient religions. Dancing is the crying outreach of the body to merge with the holy spirit. Religious dances are a form of transcendence which puts its participants in touch with other planes, dimensions, and higher states of consciousness.

Random Thoughts from the Cosmos

Most of man's pain, anxiety, and frustration come from his involvements with other people — a conflict of different self-interests. But what would life be without such involvements? It appears sometimes you are cursed if you do get involved and you are cursed if you don't. But why not give it your best shot? Otherwise, you may live a life as a lonely recluse. Everything generally works out if you look at these involvements as learning experiences and don't become too emotionally attached to them. They will even reside in the psyche long after death, for they will form the matrix for certain talents and predispositions for another incarnation.

The Christian church of today has to a large extent reached the same degree of depredation as did its Jewish counterpart. Whenever laws, decrees, rituals, observances, festivities, tithing, organization, and church buildings become more important than love and charity, then there is very little of the church worth preserving. Perhaps it still has some value as a social institution and to provide some moral and ethical guidelines for human behavior.

Random Thoughts from the Cosmos

Practicing psychiatrists and psychologists lose their perspective on normalcy and reality by their constant association with negative, neurotic, and unhappy people who cannot seem to cope with their problems. One of the biggest problems facing the profession is they cannot always change the attitudes of those whom their clients must associate with during the course of the day. Friends, family, and associates must also be willing to change in some small measure themselves. In fact, they may be the main contributors to the patient's mental anguish and instability.

Random Thoughts from the Cosmos

Does man have free will? The mere fact that one has a choice does not necessarily prove that one could have made any choice other than the one he or she made. Most choices are based on emotional considerations rather than rational. Such emotional stimuli has been programmed into us minute by minute, day by day, and year by year from the time we were born in ways which are no longer discernible to human consciousness.

Random Thoughts from the Cosmos

If Jesus Christ were to incarnate today and dwell amongst us, and he were to knock on your door, would he be invited inside or would he be rejected on the basis that you had done nothing outstanding in life to be worthy of such an honorable house call?

Since a vast majority have preconceived ideas as to what Christ would look like and what he would say, they would slam the door in his face and denounce him as an impostor — just another hippy who is opposed to war and against the present-day establishment.

Random Thoughts from the Cosmos

It's hard to love a philosopher, for he is
a metaphysical speculator who relishes
the opportunity to thrust his wisdom
upon others. Most of which is obscured
by dichotomies, paradoxes, abstractions,
and generalities. He has little or no
concern about whether he can even earn
a living doing the thing he enjoys doing
most — challenging others to examine
some of their most cherished beliefs and
opinions.

Random Thoughts from the Cosmos

If you think television and movies are
violent, we should forbid our children
from reading the Bible. Throughout the
Bible people are being stoned to death for
one reason right after another. Why
would God permit Herod to slay all the
children two years and under in an
effort to kill baby Jesus? How would
this Biblical story play out in a telecast
or in the movies? The Bible is filled
with atrocities in which innocent people
are killed merely because they were of a
different tribe or faith. God ordered his
faithful followers to kill because it
pleased Him. We know from Biblical
movies any number of innocent people
who had to be killed merely to produce a
great mythical leader.

Random Thoughts from the Cosmos

From what edition and in what language should the Bible be literally interpreted?

Random Thoughts from the Cosmos

*Opportunity knocks the loudest when
your competitor has dropped his guard
and complacency has set in.*

Random Thoughts from the Cosmos

If the dead could speak, would not some soldier ask, "What freedom is there for the man who lost his life to preserve it for others?"

Random Thoughts from the Cosmos

Every man carries around with him a concealed weapon. It's called the human mind. Every once in a while it misfires whenever he opens his mouth and exposes some of his philosophy of life. It generally takes, however, an outside stimulus to trigger that response. It could even cost him his life if some religious fanatic found his philosophy of life offensive. But why worry about it? The poor philosopher could be killed crossing an intersection or die of secondary tobacco smoke long before his enemy decides to do him in. Yes, indeed, when it's your time to go, it's your time. You more than likely will die of something you feared the least.

Random Thoughts from the Cosmos

Never tell people you love them, if they feel unworthy of love or have low self-esteem, they will find it difficult to accept your love as being sincere.

Random Thoughts from the Cosmos

Reporting the daily or weekly news is merely one man's opinion as to what occurred. What really happens is seldom authenticated by anyone directly involved in the incident or skirmish. While the tabloids are reckless with the truth and the facts, even your conventional magazines and newspapers seldom verify the source and accuracy of what they print. For instance, who has tried to verify the statistical data gathered by the EPA as to how many people died of secondary tobacco smoke (3,000) or did we accept it because we assumed our government wouldn't have any reason to lie to us about such a critical health issue? The government lies to us all the time to divert our attention from the critical issues to those which we can personally do something about, which are trivial by comparison to the big problems facing this nation.

Random Thoughts from the Cosmos

It's not what I said that counts, it's what you think I said.

Random Thoughts from the Cosmos

Gossip is subject to embellishment to keep the listener from getting bored.

Random Thoughts from the Cosmos

What's wrong with the younger generation? Mostly, the older generation. They seem to have forgotten how it felt to be young, free, and uninhibited. It is the older generation who is primarily responsible for passing all these ordinances against drugs, alcohol, tobacco, and pornography and who want to make Christian robots out of their children. The older generations had the freedom to experiment, which is no longer tolerable in our present day society. Kids are bored today because of all the restrictions placed on them thus stifling their creativity and their need for adventure. It now appears that the cure (harsher punishment) is worse than the disease (restraints placed on their rights to make choices).

Random Thoughts from the Cosmos

We have independent Certified Public Accounting firms who audit private businesses to protect the interests of owners or stockholders from fraud and dishonesty. And yet the largest corporate stockholder is the American taxpayer, and yet he has no way of employing an independent accounting firm to hold the government accountable for truth and honesty. True, the U.S., state, and local governments have internal auditing systems, but the problem is they are, nonetheless, government employees who will seldom blow the whistle on a superior. If they do blow it, they could be asked to quit rather than be fired. If your superiors want to lie to the American people, you better not challenge the powers that be. People will lie about almost anything if it will make them look good or advance their career.

Random Thoughts from the Cosmos

Rebelliousness by youth is oftentimes a desperate attempt by children to get the attention of their parents who are so preoccupied with social, lodge, church and business commitments that they have little or no time for their kids. One of the biggest problems with our society is we punish children for their disruptive behavior when it is frequently caused by parental abuse and neglect. Society plays a big role and is equally responsible for juvenile delinquency as its attitude has shifted from rehabilitation, mercy, empathy, and leniency to that of maximum punishment because society is convinced it acts as a deterrent when, in fact, it's an invitation for more antisocial behavior and rebelliousness.

Random Thoughts from the Cosmos

Rebels lay the ground work for change, but politicians get the credit — if they are able to act in time. Only too often politicians wake up too late to avoid a revolution of major proportions.

Random Thoughts from the Cosmos

How readily one forgets his promises to God. Chances are He wasn't listening anyway. Sometimes things do work out for the best even when we forget to pray and act on our own behalf without ever asking God for His permission or blessing. We may, at a later time, give Him all the credit at some church testimonial if things turn out favorably even though we acted on our own at the time. It adds a little tinge of humility to our act if we give God all the credit. Whenever God fails to answer our prayers, however, no mention is ever made of the fact. We are somewhat reluctant to testify about the numerous times God disappointed us, since we wouldn't want him to appear namby-pamby.

Random Thoughts from the Cosmos

Whenever the political party with which we are affiliated does something that meets with our approval, we will read every word about it in the newspaper with great interest, otherwise, we turn to the sports page, comics, or entertainment sections first. Most of the time, however, we never bother going back to read or analyze anything which goes against our political or religious philosophy. Sometimes we get so emotionally attached to our political and religious views, we lose our ability to reason.

Random Thoughts from the Cosmos

Whenever secondary tobacco smoke is considered to be more hazardous to life and limb than breaking the speed limit or owning guns, then we have lost our ability to reason logically. No one can prove that secondary tobacco smoke causes cancer anymore than they can attribute it to radiation, car emissions, or industrial pollution. The secondary tobacco scare was initiated by the EPA, the AMA, and the Surgeon General in order to justify their existence and the huge salaries they pay their executives and directors. How many of these agencies have any direct-daily contact with individual physicians from which they supposedly compile their statistical data?

Random Thoughts from the Cosmos

New ideas put a hold on old age.

Random Thoughts from the Cosmos

If the poor and middle class keep getting poorer, then how are the rich going to get richer unless they devise a scheme as to how they can take some of the money away from those who are now in their own economic class?

Random Thoughts from the Cosmos

Let's worry a little less about civil rights violations in other countries and focus a little more on the injustices and inequities in our own. The media likes to direct our attention elsewhere in order to divert our awareness away from the problems here at home. Don't tell me what's going on in Bosnia, let's hear about what's transpiring in Mississippi, Michigan, Ohio, etc. Just maybe, there are some hot spots here in our own country which are very close to being out of control, which get little or no media attention if they are not within our state or region.

Random Thoughts from the Cosmos

There are two types of time — objective and subjective or they may be identified as real or psychological. Psychological time is not measured by hours and minutes but relative to the intensity of one's aches and pains or the happiness derived by engaging in pleasurable activities. Did you ever notice how fast time slips by when you are totally engrossed in doing something you thoroughly enjoy?

Random Thoughts from the Cosmos

Two enemies who discover they have a common enemy may soon have a basis for becoming good friends.

Random Thoughts from the Cosmos

Many who attend church appear to be
hypocrites when, in fact, they are still in
the evaluation stage trying to decide if
they can find some basis upon which
they can really and truly say,
"I believe." In the meantime, their lives
have to go on pretty much the way it did
before they became churchgoers. Besides,
it's not all that easy to give up your
sinful lifestyle. The real hypocrite is the
one who goes around trying to convert
others before he or she is convinced that
the Bible is 100% true. He still may be
trying to resolve the question as to
whether Biblical truths can be justified
on faith alone when they are contrary to
scientific theory and facts.

Random Thoughts from the Cosmos

I have asked several ministers and devout layman what justification could there be for God taking the life of a small child either by disease or by accident? Invariably, the answer was the same as I received from the many other questions asked during the course of my life. The most common reply was: "We don't have all the answers."

What are my unexpressed thoughts and feelings when I hear that type of response? "If you don't have all the answers, how can you be so positive that you have any of the answers? Does that give the ministry the right to seek legislation for imposing their religious values upon me when they admit they don't have all the answers?"

Random Thoughts from the Cosmos

Sometimes tears are our way of showing others how unfair life has been to us and how terrible wrongs have been inflicted upon us by those who were heartless, selfish, ruthless, and cruel. Many times those tears are, in fact, caused by feeling sorry for ourselves for being so gullible and susceptible to those who were insincere if not downright dishonest.

Compromise is often worse than defeat, for it allows the other party to share in the victory celebration.

Random Thoughts from the Cosmos

You'll never be much more than what you are now by associating solely with those in your own peer group.

Random Thoughts from the Cosmos

Most of us get trapped in the back waters and stagnant pools of life — afraid to venture out to the surging main stream which could provide us with some new challenges and an opportunity to see some new scenery. Some will venture out into the rapids a wee bit too far unprepared to meet the onrushing current.

Suggestion: Anticipate some of the problems and be prepared for the worse. If you can forge the stream to the other side, there may be some vistas and surprises to make it well worth the effort. Chart the course with care and you will be ecstatic in your moment of triumph. It's better to take a few risks than die of boredom.

Random Thoughts from the Cosmos

*Every time I sit down to have a little talk
with myself, there is a part of me who
wants to talk back.*

Random Thoughts from the Cosmos

Humility is the painful aftermath of discovering that someone beat you at your own game.

Random Thoughts from the Cosmos

Nothing in life is free — not even salvation. Remember the preacher has to make a living too. He's not in the ministry just for the fun of it nor will he be content to work for a minimum wage.

Random Thoughts from the Cosmos

God would like to see a little less preaching about salvation and a little more emphasis upon love. Love without social action and gratuities for the poor and needy is but a vain word that has no substance.

Random Thoughts from the Cosmos

The older generation has no understanding of the impact technology and urbanization has had upon the younger generation. It appears that there is no social contact or dialogue between the two. I am not sure that grandparents or even parents have any empathy for the younger generation as we keep imposing more and more restrictions upon their behavior. I'm not even sure the young people can analyze the causes for their restlessness, discontent, and rebellion. Most of the problems of the younger people are caused by their families, churches, and law enforcement agencies, which harasses the younger generation and curtails many of their activities. Those who control this society are more focused on obedience and punishment than on love, compassion, and understanding.

Random Thoughts from the Cosmos

Should one have to pay insurance premiums on the hospital bill of a skier who gets hurt or killed on the slopes or skids off the highway on a snow packed road only to kill or mangle some innocent party who was a nonskier. Tell me how that is different from paying the hospital bill of one who is dying from lung cancer because of his addiction to tobacco or some innocent party dying of secondary tobacco smoke. How about the innocent party hurt or killed in an auto accident by a driver who was driving faster than the speed limit? Let's make it illegal to drive automobiles because some innocent party gets killed? Is it fair to compare secondary tobacco with speeding or skiing fatalities? Perhaps all I can afford are the simple pleasures of life like a pack of cigarettes and my glass of beer at the local pub.

Random Thoughts from the Cosmos

A friend is one who understands us well
enough to know that we are inclined to
say things at times that we really don't
mean. We all have those kinds of days
when a little bit of jealousy, stress,
anxiety, frustration, envy, or resentment
just seems to creep into our conversation
and our rage erupts into a tirade of
words unleashing a lot of pent up
feelings or emotions. When we look back
at our behavior, we are somewhat
mystified as to the precise causes.

Random Thoughts from the Cosmos

If there was ever a time for Jesus Christ to make his reappearance, now is the time. Man has made such a mess of his ability to bring order and harmony out of chaos, you would think it's time for God to intervene. If Christ returns, one would hope that he would bring with him an all new Bible written not in stone (as were the ten commandments) but in English on the finest parchment. Maybe he will descend from a UFO and immediately set to work healing millions who have no medical insurance.

Christ's return to earth has been predicted for nearly two thousand years. With satellites Christ could have a worldwide television audience. Then he would have an opportunity to make believers out of every one. The problem would be that it would take hundreds of interpreters to translate his messages.

Random Thoughts from the Cosmos

Most people know what a placebo is. It is commonly referred to as the sugar pill. They use placebos mostly in medical research when experimenting with new drugs. In research you have two control groups. You give a new drug to half the group and a sugar pill to the other half to see if it has any curative effects. If the half who took the new drug had significant results, the drug is marketed. But some who took the sugar pill got well also, which proves that the power of the mind has the ability to cure as well. Conversely, very few people were ever bothered by secondary tobacco smoke until the AMA and the government kept reinforcing our belief over a number of years that secondary tobacco smoke surely would kill us all. Many of our allergies are psychologically induced.

Random Thoughts from the Cosmos

To reason things logically will thwart us emotionally causing all sorts of anxieties and frustrations. Try getting your intellect and your emotions in sync sometime. It can be a real struggle between the wills.

Random Thoughts from the Cosmos

A real friend is one who will defend you in the presence of others when you are not around.

Random Thoughts from the Cosmos

God knows everything, but He ain't talking about how to solve the world's problems — or at least not since He sent Jesus Christ down to straighten things out. It may be a little early to tell if He was successful, but it doesn't look too encouraging. God may, however, have to send another reluctant messenger who will not accept the assignment cheerfully knowing how complex the world is today compared with what it was back 2000 years ago. This poor soul will be without credentials, endorsements, or a public relations staff. He will be strictly on his own. Of course, every effort will be made to prove he is a sinner and not a saint — a man and not a god.

Random Thoughts from the Cosmos

A conference or a board of director's meeting is a formal meeting where most of the time will be spent deciding what is going to be tabled until the next scheduled meeting.

Random Thoughts from the Cosmos

Most people will buy any philosophy that promises a "full stomach" and a greater share of the world's material goods and wealth or maybe, I should say, a disproportionate share.

Random Thoughts from the Cosmos

Many of the nice things a person said about a departed love one are often retracted after the will is read.

Random Thoughts from the Cosmos

Please, I beg of you, don't drive your car! Take a bus or the rapid transit to work. It is true some people are smokers, but it's hardly worth mentioning compared to secondary auto emissions and industrial pollutants which infiltrate your lungs causing cancer and other respiratory diseases. Don't breathe other people's germs as they are hazardous to your health. Always wear a protective face mask to insure longevity of life if for no other reason than to protect yourself from pollutants, chemicals and germs. Just one more thing — Be sure to wear bullet proof clothing because you might get hit by a stray bullet. Why take chances? Be sure you watch your fat and cholesterol intake. Things which you like or enjoy doing aren't worth the risk. So you die of boredom bound by the rules of social and religious propriety.

Random Thoughts from the Cosmos

*People who are steadfast in their refusal
to play the other man's game generally
end up playing solitaire.*

Random Thoughts from the Cosmos

Male chauvinism is slowly declining now that women possess most of the world's wealth.

Random Thoughts from the Cosmos

Every year we keep passing more and more laws and ordinances to prohibit certain types of behavior. The more laws we pass, the more crime we have. Getting tough on crime has only caused our prison population to double over the past ten years. Stiffer prison sentences have done nothing to deter crime. The more laws we pass, the more juveniles rebel against society. But if you think crime is out of control now, wait until we do away with the welfare system.

Random Thoughts from the Cosmos

Satirical Commentary

God is not always right, but He is, nonetheless, God; and the odds are all on his side. Sorry, but God has no Court of Appeals. He is a one man Supreme Court. Prostrate yourself before God Almighty that He might show you some mercy and consideration on judgment day — you wretched sinner. If you appease Him and try to please Him, He probably will have even less respect and tolerance for a sniveling coward than had there been an open confrontation. One would think God might have some admiration for those who have the courage to speak out against some of the injustices in this world. God must find life pretty boring without some opposition.

Random Thoughts from the Cosmos

People who have found it relatively easy to achieve their goals because of their good looks, well-developed physiques, and radiant personalities often find as they approach old age that they have depleted some of their natural resources.

Random Thoughts from the Cosmos

Politics is merely a game of how the power and wealth should be redistributed. Should the artificially generated money (printing money and accruing a federal deficit) be given to the wealthy or the poor? Some Europeans believe that American Capitalism is Socialism for the wealthy and the government is draining the poor and middle classes to pay for the losses incurred by the large depositors of banks and S & Ls whose accounts are guaranteed by the F.D.I.C. The private banks, (solely free-enterprise businesses), are using the federal income tax paid by the lower income groups to finance the losses incurred by the wealthy. If that isn't socialism for the upper income classes, what is it?

Random Thoughts from the Cosmos

Many a man and woman have been spurred to success by being spurned by his or her lover. You know the old "I'll-show-him-a-thing-or-two" attitude. Then you have those who seek revenge and retaliate with vengeance equal to the fury of God. The first approach is generally more gratifying in the long run.

Random Thoughts from the Cosmos

Within one month's time, I read in one newspaper that the EPA reported that 3,000 people died of secondary tobacco every year. In yet another newspaper, I read that 30,000 people died of secondary tobacco smoke. In neither case did it mention the individual's name who was responsible for the dissemination of these statistics. What agency did the EPA contact to get such information? Anytime government warns you about something — beware! It is a ploy used for political purposes — usually to appease the voters of the powerful Christian Coalition. The EPA says nothing, however, about the number of people who die each year of lung cancer caused by auto emissions and industrial pollutants.

Random Thoughts from the Cosmos

Once a friend starts being critical of others and complains about everyone and every petty flaw in the societal fabric, there is little if anything to be lost in defending those who aren't present to defend themselves. Besides, I don't need friends who can't see another person's point of view. Most of the time you can see why others think and behave as they do if you had any knowledge of their personal and environmental backgrounds. In fact, you would, in all probability, think and behave exactly the same way had you lived under identical circumstances. If this statement has any merit, how could you not love your enemies?

Random Thoughts from the Cosmos

A friendship or a marriage lasts only as long as both parties derive some mutual gratification from the relationship or else one or the other might see, looming on the horizon, some opportunities to better themselves by separating.

Random Thoughts from the Cosmos

One's hatred for another is frequently as intense as was his or her love.

Random Thoughts from the Cosmos

Unfortunately, apologies are held by a vast segment of this society to be a sign of weakness or lack of conviction. We all have our moments of frustration when we angrily vent our frustrations, anxieties, and disappointments by taking our hostilities out on our friends, members of the family, and acquaintances merely because of their accessibility. Very seldom do they understand why they're the target of our rage. Hopefully, they will see the source of our irritation and understand. Otherwise, those of us who are guilty of such deviant behavior may have to find an explanation or offer an apology.

Random Thoughts from the Cosmos

Apologies are generally offered when you want to preserve a relationship which you feel still has some worthwhile and mutual benefits worth salvaging.

Random Thoughts from the Cosmos

The future is often beclouded by our expectations that history will repeat itself.

Random Thoughts from the Cosmos

If you have very few or no friends at all, it could be a result of your general unwillingness to change some of your beliefs, ideas, and opinions. If that doesn't make a difference, maybe you should change some of your habits or appearance.

Random Thoughts from the Cosmos

One of the hardest disciplines anyone has to acquire is learning to divide his time so he can spend a proportional amount among work, family, and his own personal hobbies and recreational pursuits.

Random Thoughts from the Cosmos

If you are going to be a winner, you can't afford to spend most of your time with losers. The problem is learning to spot a winner. A financial success may be a winner in one sense of the word, but a loser in the intellectual, social, and cultural areas of life. So what kind of winner are you striving to emulate?

Random Thoughts from the Cosmos

The politicians we send to Washington place their own self-interests ahead of the electorate. They have to make it big while they are in office and they have to be able change their position according to the latest polls. After all, where can a politician find a high paying executive position in the private sector once he has been fired by the electorate? He has to be able to gauge how the political winds will blow and then try to second-guess what public opinion will be relative to the issues come election time. If he doesn't make enough money while in office to retire after a couple of terms, he probably can't be rehabilitated for any useful-type employment in the free-enterprise sector.

Random Thoughts from the Cosmos

Personal Commentary

*The older I get the more I realize that my
father and mother didn't have all the
answers either. My father told me when
I asked him to lend me enough money to
buy a McDonald's franchise back in
1959 that they would go broke selling
hamburgers for 15 cents. That wasn't
the only thing my parents were wrong
about. I'm convinced, that in many
cases, parents should have listened to
their kids after seeing what a mess some
parents made of their own lives. I
attribute my ability to think and to
reason by the fact that I had no religious
indoctrination as a child. That was a
plus amidst many negatives. As far as
"family values", I don't remember being
taught any. I had to learn from
experience and experimentation.*

Random Thoughts from the Cosmos

Scientists haven't, as yet, been able to distinguish between an addiction and a habit. Whatever might be your compulsive disorder is an addiction. Whatever mine might be is merely a bad habit. You decide which of those listed below are bad habits and which are addictions:

- *alcohol • tobacco • religion • sweets*
- *caffeine • sex • snacking • crusading*
  - *organizational or church activities*
  - *chocolate • spectator sports • chess*
    - *bridge • poker • drugs • work*
    - *speeding • gardening • recreation*
- *hobbies • gambling • guns • cheating*
  - *television • socializing • business*
    - *investing*

Anything done to excess may be detrimental to your health or well being. So why single out tobacco?

Random Thoughts from the Cosmos

*People handle **criticism** in different ways. Some get angry. Some let it sail in one ear and out the other. Some might agree as to its validity but are unable to change anything at the present time. Some politely reject criticism and wonder about the motives of their critics. Some people feel threatened by criticism and go on the offensive. Some will merely withdraw from those offering it. And some will give it some serious consideration after scrutinizing the motives of those offering such criticism.*

Random Thoughts from the Cosmos

Keeping up with the Joneses and the Smiths presents some interesting speculation for one who might be able to do so, if he so chooses. But why buy an expensive automobile or a luxurious suburban mansion merely to impress your neighbors and friends when they are so busy trying to impress you that they have little or no time to be impressed?

Random Thoughts from the Cosmos

*The only reason I could ever love you is
because the Bible tells me to.*

Random Thoughts from the Cosmos

The validity of any criticism may be in direct proportion to the amount of anger it arouses.

Random Thoughts from the Cosmos

I am not opposed to compromising my values if I only knew what they were.

Random Thoughts from the Cosmos

Coalitions may be formed at times by the strangest and most diverse groups of people you would ever want to meet. Can you imagine what common cause could unite liberals, atheists, agnostics, humanitarians, moderate Christians, and reincarnationists? It would be to form a coalition to fight the politically oriented conservative-right-wing-fundamentalist Christians who want prayer in schools, dress codes, private schools, teaching of creation science, strong discipline, no minorities, no drugs, no sex-education courses, and sexual abstinence. These overzealous seekers of power are no longer supporters of Amendment One of our constitution. They are following the same patterns of fanaticism the Arabs have been following for centuries. The constitution was drafted to protect minority opinions and beliefs.

Random Thoughts from the Cosmos

A friend is one who is never too busy to listen to your problems, but let him suggest a solution and the relationship may be terminated immediately. In many cases, the complainer isn't seeking a solution but only looking for a little sympathy. He enjoys his "poor-me" status.

Random Thoughts from the Cosmos

Most people have more than two facades. The most noticeable facades are the difference between their business and social characterizations. There are businessmen who are convincing — but don't believe every word they say. Ministers are almost as notorious as they try to render Biblical interpretations which are compounding error upon error and interpretation upon other interpretations which has been going on for centuries. I condemn neither ministers nor businessmen, for we all have to make a living one way or another.

All I ask of the ministry is: Please don't try to impose your self-righteous rhetoric or salesmanship upon one who has played most of those word games as a businessman himself. Peace be with you brother!

Random Thoughts from the Cosmos

Possibly there is no one more dangerous than a person who has just had his ego suddenly deflated. Don't strip him of all his verbal defenses, for he may not know how to counter and will come out fighting with all his guns a blazing. He may be totally out of control. So use a little discretion in discrediting or embarrassing him. Give him a way that he can bow out gracefully.

Random Thoughts from the Cosmos

You can't make everyone love you. The next best thing is teaching others to respect you.

Random Thoughts from the Cosmos

What do people do who don't smoke or drink alcohol to relax when they are burdened with anxieties, frustrations, fears, financial problems, hostility, or abuse? There are some who find release and relief by attacking those who smoke and drink by forming an aggressive coalition to seek legislation to put a halt to drinking and smoking in parks, at sports arenas, or any other public facilities. However, many of these do-gooders are not opposed to ownership of guns. It's all right to kill innocent people with a gun but not from alcohol. Nobody is expressing any great interest in outlawing handguns or automatic weapons. Look at the death toll each year of people killed with fire arms compared to the 3,000 people the EPA claims dies of secondary tobacco smoke, which cannot even be verified. It's just so much propaganda.

Random Thoughts from the Cosmos

I could have a great deal of compassion for those who suffer in silence, if I but knew who they were. There must be lots of them out there judging from the few friends and acquaintances whom I have encouraged to talk about their personal lives. They have been more than willing to share their personal problems and grievances with me. You see, they are pretty well convinced theirs are far more serious than anyone else, but having talked to many strangers, I am convinced everyone has problems — even the wealthy. Strangers are more likely to open up and tell you things they would not tell their closest friends. Where do you meet these strangers? At coffee-shop counters, bars, and church socials.

Random Thoughts from the Cosmos

All rules, laws, and regulations are subject to interpretation by the boss.

Random Thoughts from the Cosmos

What happens to the soul of a fetus which has been aborted? It will find another mother and another fetus to inhabit prior to birth. Contrary to what Christians teach, most souls do not enter the fetus immediately upon conception. Some do not enter until several months prior to birth. A choice as to which mother a soul will be born is usually a matter of the soul's choice. Sometimes, however, parental commitments were made prior to the birth of either parent. There is such a thing as group karma.

Random Thoughts from the Cosmos

In conversing with others in coffee shops, bars, and discussion groups, it has been interesting to note the large number of people who are opposed to both abortion and welfare. They believe a soul has a right to life even if there is a high degree of probability that many of the new born will have a standard of living far below the poverty level. Maybe the anti-abortionists will have to reincarnate in another life to experience homelessness and hunger.

Random Thoughts from the Cosmos

To have an inferiority complex isn't all that bad. In fact, it gives you a slight edge, for you realize you have to work a little harder and rely a little more on your imagination and creative ingenuity to get the kind of recognition and monetary return you feel you deserve.

Random Thoughts from the Cosmos

The question has arisen time and time again for people who believe in reincarnation as to why there are more people on the face of the earth than there has ever been before. There are a number of answers to that question. First, is that when people die, they do not reincarnate immediately but dwell in other dimensions and even on other planets where their planetary time is quite different from earth time. While residing there, they may live to be a thousand years old in earth time. Second, there are dimensions where souls live where time is nonexistent. It's much like a dream in that you are unaware of the passage of time. Some souls have been earthlings many times while others but a few.

Random Thoughts from the Cosmos

Do the strong have compassion for the weak, the rich for the poor, the healthy for the sick, the abstainer for the alcoholic, the nonsmoker for the smoker, the young for the old, the religious for the atheist or agnostic, whites for the blacks, the winner for the loser, the executive for the union laborer, the genius for those of average intelligence, the victim for the criminal? What was Christ's message of love all about anyway? Only by the grace of God are you not walking in some other man's shoes. (Sometimes, I even get a small ego boost after being so tolerant and a feeling of being divine when I realize that I belong to such a small minority of liberals).

Random Thoughts from the Cosmos

Some people have few friends because they are convinced that everyone is using them to achieve their own particular ends. Maybe you can turn their game into one that is mutually beneficial to both parties.

Random Thoughts from the Cosmos

One can become a loser with very little effort — just refuse to change some of your habits and beliefs in an ever changing world.

Random Thoughts from the Cosmos

Adults have gangs also. They call them coalitions. Coalitions seek to take rights and privileges away from those whose moral values do not coincide with their own. In a sense, they are beating up on those who don't agree with them. Adults set the stage for juvenile violence.

Random Thoughts from the Cosmos

Most Americans believe Socialism and Communism are one and the same. The basic difference is that people who live in the Socialist countries own their own homes, automobiles, and privately-owned businesses. What are some of these countries? They are Denmark, Sweden, Norway, Germany, France, Finland, etc. The Socialist countries appear to be more concerned about the general welfare of their own countrymen than most Americans. Most Americans, I observe, put self interests ahead of what is best for the country, which will ultimately destroy it.

Random Thoughts from the Cosmos

Mediocrity is not as fatal a condition as it might appear, for most of us can do something about it. If not, we generally have enough intelligence to conceal the fact we aren't the brightest or the cleverest people in the world. Sometimes, however, those of us of lesser intelligence, can fool even the most scholarly and perceptive observers. Even those who are mediocre at most things can excel at something. All you have to do is to keep people's attention focused on your strongest talent or suit.

Random Thoughts from the Cosmos

I hear God is having trouble with some of His staff. It seems there are several angels who are challenging His authority. There is always another Lucifer testing and trying the patience of God to see if he can get a majority vote in the King's court. Many of the angels think it's about time for a whole new regime. After all, the job is too big for one man, not even a computer whiz could keep pace with all the changes. Of course, nothing ever gets done until everything falls completely apart and the revolution is underway — be it on the ethereal or earthly plane. The angelic hosts seem to have lost all contact with the White House and Congress in Washington, D.C. and are seeking new means to communicate.

Random Thoughts from the Cosmos

I got tired of being thirty-nine and holding once I heard that life begins at forty.

Random Thoughts from the Cosmos

Strict obedience to family rules with frequent threats of punishment when those rules are disobeyed, will produce a neurotic and rebellious child when there are no rewards or gratuities given for compliance. Children must sense the presence of love, concern, and unity among family members or else dissension and rebellion will persist when they are away from their home environment. Remember how a dog trainer gives his animal a treat after each successful performance of a trick? Children have to be equally compensated. All punishment and no rewards will create a delinquent and violent child who is not only out to humiliate his parents but to show his contempt for the rest of society.

Random Thoughts from the Cosmos

Once you have made a mistake, don't dwell on it. It's all right to analyze it and try to figure out where you might have gone wrong, but then lay it aside. Turn your back on the past without bitterness or resentment, and release it to the Cosmos.

Random Thoughts from the Cosmos

When someone is angry with you, that's not the time to tell him about his faults and shortcomings. It's a sure way to lose a friend. But not all is lost, for even if you should have the courage to tell him, you may learn something about yourself. If you stopped to analyze the situation, you learned the importance of being discreet — a lesson which you would not otherwise have had the opportunity to experience. You can always find another friend. There is always a positive side to every negative encounter.

Random Thoughts from the Cosmos

If you believe in a personal God, you surely must realize that He can't always answer your prayers. Remember, He has to do a lot of manipulation of others, which is depriving them of their free will, before He can fulfill your request. God doesn't like taking sides but frequently He has no choice. But why should God always cast his lot on your behalf when there are as many earnest, sincere, hardworking, and moral people as you who deserve equal consideration? Then you must be prepared to become the target of His manipulation in helping the other party to have his prayers answered. It sounds absurd but it gives you something to think about if your prayers go unfulfilled. I guess I'm simply not smart enough to figure out how all this prayer business works and I probably never will.

Random Thoughts from the Cosmos

What happens when two sincere and devout Christians pray for different outcomes? One man may pray that he be allowed to die thus ridding himself of all this pain and anguish which he has endured in his old age. A relative, on the other hand, may pray that he be allowed to go on living — often for very selfish reasons. So whose prayer is going to be answered? Someone is surely going to be disappointed. It's hard to say whose prayers are going to be answered for God does things in such a whimsical and arbitrary way.

Random Thoughts from the Cosmos

After Christians leave church on Sunday, they seldom take God home with them. It's business as usual until the following Sunday.

Random Thoughts from the Cosmos

*Poverty does nothing to strengthen
man's faith in God.*

Random Thoughts from the Cosmos

The fate of this country lies not within the jurisdiction of God but with its politicians, industrialists, the Federal Reserve, the banks, the investment and brokerage firms, and the multimillion dollar enterprise known as the Christian Coalition embraced by the other big-time TV evangelists.

What I can't figure out is: Who is the Master Manipulator who coordinates all these activities? Maybe the Master Manipulator isn't free of being manipulated by some little guys at the very bottom of the ladder who have aspirations of their own, which are quite unsettling for the big-time-power brokers.

Random Thoughts from the Cosmos

The problem with a democracy that allows free speech, the right to assemble, and the right to bear arms is that it always has a group of people who will take full advantage of these freedoms to destroy the very country which gave them those rights to begin with.

Random Thoughts from the Cosmos

Children are the scapegoats for everything that's wrong in this world. They are the product of a society which has far too many ordinances and laws — all passed by adults to keep kids from experimenting and disallowing them the freedom to find out what good and evil are all about. The price kids have to pay for experimentation with illegal substances is excessive. Children will be stashed away in some jail or prison without ever being rehabilitated for civilian life. We just keep passing more laws as a measure of social control. Lighten up on the penalties for using drugs, alcohol, tobacco, and pornography, and many will lose all interest in them since they will no longer be illegal or taboo.

Random Thoughts from the Cosmos

The problem with liberals is that they are not fighters. They will sit idly by and allow the conservatives to banish their basic rights and freedoms. Most liberals don't even own a gun. Somehow the word "liberal" has taken on a meaning which is just the opposite of what it used to be. If you don't like someone just call them a liberal. People were once proud of the fact they were liberals. Now they are considered to be that bunch of radicals who support Amendment One rights in the Constitution. Perhaps liberals deserve what they get. They are so liberal as to stand idly by and let the conservatives take away their basic freedoms.

Random Thoughts from the Cosmos

To make a mistake once is ignorance, but to make the same mistake continuously is a sign of stupidity. It's not that you are exactly dumb. Chances are either you are letting your emotions control your decision making processes or there are some basic flaws in your beliefs or logic.

Random Thoughts from the Cosmos

If the saints and saviors can't save the world, maybe we should turn it over to a common sinner. At least the sinner might have a little compassion for the poor, the mentally retarded, the elderly, the homeless, the disabled, and those who weren't born with the intelligence to excel. There is very little in church budgets for humanitarian aid, and what little has been budgeted is mostly for foreign missions. Most churches are not welfare agencies. The main thrust of their gospel is focused on morals and salvation. They preach fear and guilt rather than love, forgiveness, and tolerance. Their focus is more on hate than love.

Random Thoughts from the Cosmos

Not every one is a liar by intention. He is probably quoting some well-known authority or expert on a subject which this poor, unsuspecting soul knows very little about, and that should be considered a forgivable sin. It is difficult at times to forgive a person who says, states, or infers that anyone who isn't a Christian is doomed to perdition. As one who has reason to believe that reincarnation is a fact, I refute their doctrine of salvation by grace. It would be fitting, however, if those who preach such doctrines could be allowed to spend some time in Hell to find out if it is a permanent condition. Chances are they will discover sooner or later, they are now living in Hell as residents of the planet Earth.

Random Thoughts from the Cosmos

Adolescents take drugs to escape the hypocrisy they see in their homes, churches, courts, schools, and in the business world. This is to say nothing about the way judges hand out long sentences to youthful offenders who haven't lived long enough to have the necessary experiences or exposure to make rational judgments. Those judges have little or no knowledge of human nature and how they actually contribute to the rebellion of our youth. If Jesus Christ were to return tomorrow (assuming that He could), I'm sure he would be appalled by the intolerant and judgmental souls claiming to be Christians.

Random Thoughts from the Cosmos

Truth is camouflaged by abstract words and terminology as truth can be interpreted to mean whatever you want it to mean. The Bible says, "Thou shalt not kill." The thing is that you can murder someone just as easily with words as you can with bullets. Let's call it psychological abuse, whereby, by constantly reminding others about their inadequacies, incompetency, and inconsistencies, we can destroy their self-confidence and faith in their ability to compete in the world of commerce. Psychological abuse affects one's physical health thus shortening human life. Does shortening another person's life constitute murder? In that case, maybe we are all murderers.

Random Thoughts from the Cosmos

People turn their "wish" lists over to God and pray that He will intercede on their behalf. Most Christians pray for what they want rather than what's good for them.

Random Thoughts from the Cosmos

Politicians and religious leaders have had us so focused on the evils of tobacco, alcohol, drugs, and pornography that we forgot all about the really big problems which confront this nation — quality health care, homelessness, hunger, neglected children, crime, physical abuse, crooked politicians, minimum wages, disobedience of the law, immigration, and education. Our leaders try to divert our attention away from the important issues of the day by focusing on inconsequential and trivial matters to cover up for their ineptitude to solve the really big problems confronting this nation.

Random Thoughts from the Cosmos

The industrialists and many of the politicians led us to believe that one of the reasons why hard and soft goods cost so much is the high cost of labor. They led us to believe that if the country could only rid itself of labor unions, it would greatly reduce the cost of domestic goods, and the savings would be passed on to the consumer. For the most part labor unions are now a thing of the past, but prices have continued to spiral upwards. The savings in labor costs only put more profit in the pockets of the industrialists and the stockholders.

The question is: Who is going to buy the big-ticket-hard goods when the working man can no longer afford anything more than the necessities of life?

Random Thoughts from the Cosmos

The lonely sheep herder probably feels closer to God than those who go to church. At least there is no one trying to make him believe something which isn't necessarily the truth. Nature is his cathedral where words are totally unnecessary, for he can feel God's presence in a world where there are no lies, deception, greed, distractions, or competition.

Random Thoughts from the Cosmos

Sometimes it becomes necessary to discard old friends who have become set in their ways and stagnant in their ways of thinking.

Random Thoughts from the Cosmos

Oh yes! There is always that remote possibility that I might be wrong, but I'm about as close to perfection as I'm ever going to get.

Random Thoughts from the Cosmos

Why do we put such a high price tag on life when heaven is just around the corner? Why are we so concerned about winning and saving souls for Christ, when all we have to do is live a pure and simple life by adhering to those morals and principles which the Bible teaches us to honor? Why are we trying so hard to make converts when all we have to do is believe? Why go on living when we will be reunited ultimately with friends and family in heaven(provided, of course, they are saved when they die)? Then there will be that reconciliation with our enemies who, somehow, managed to get saved also. They will be more amiable and agreeable than they ever were here on earth.

Random Thoughts from the Cosmos
Some Political Reforms needed in the U.S.A.

- *Abolishing the two house system*
- *One chamber — based on population alone*
- *Multi-party system — preferably five or six parties*
- *A steeply graduated income tax*
- *Doubling the size of the House of Representatives as you will be doing away with the Senate*
- *Government lending money to farmers to start co-ops to process and retail food from crops they raise — too many middle men in the marketing chain.*
- *Repeal all laws restricting individual's rights to make choices on matters of ethics and morality*
- *Legalize drugs, pornography, and prostitution*
- *Allow some public beaches for nude bathing*
- *Enforce anti-trust laws*
- *Provide public housing for the poor and needy where they can raise their own crops or take the transit to the city where they can get a job*
- *Print money without incurring debt to finance social programs and using price controls if necessary to control inflation.*
- *Humanizing the penal system*
- *Provide airtight and well ventilated rooms for*

Random Thoughts from the Cosmos

smokers in large public and privately owned office buildings.
• Rebuild the passenger rail system across the U.S.A.
• Rapid transit system for metropolitan areas
• Creating jobs using the unemployed by building high speed trains for rural areas
• Prohibit congressional lobbying in all state and federal chambers.
• Do away with large corporate donations and PACS.
• No term limits on a multi-party system
• Legalize abortion
• Owners of private businesses will decide whether smoking will be allowed in their buildings or place of business. Let the owners of a restaurant or bar make the decision as to whether smoking will be permitted in their businesses while making it illegal for nonsmoking coalitions from harassing owners by threats or intimidation if they don't go nonsmoking.
• Minimum wage adjusted annually to include cost of living index.
• All utilities would be owned by local, state, or federal government.
• All churches and religious organizations would pay personal property and income taxes.

Random Thoughts from the Cosmos

• *All parks owned by the city, county, state, or federal governments will have no admission fees since they are supported by all the taxpayers.*
• *All coliseums, stadiums, and auditoriums shall be built by private corporations and will be assessed taxes thereon letting the purchaser of tickets pay for the cost of the building, maintenance, upkeep, and all expenses related thereto rather than using taxpayer's money.*
• *Ban all assault weapons*
• *Registration of all guns*
• *Personal property taxes will be levied on all individual or corporate assets to pay for the national defense budget.*
• *Separation of church and state*
• *No prayers in public schools*
• *Publicly-owned facilities cannot be leased to religious organizations or churches.*
• *A bigger federal government to insure equitable rights among all the states; otherwise let's make each state a separate country — there are too many subdivisions of government with conflicting laws between federal, state, county, and municipalities*
• *Hesitate in changing government too fast or too radically or else a revolution will follow.*

Random Thoughts from the Cosmos

A child who truly loves his parents will imitate their behavioral patterns and accept their values. The question is, "How do you get a child's attention and cooperation?"

Random Thoughts from the Cosmos

Life is full of frustrations, trials,
obstacles, reversals, delays, anxieties,
detours, disappointments, repressions,
accidents, untimely deaths, natural
disasters, and victims of unusual
happenings. Most of these cause some
measure of anger at ourselves, others, or
even at God. The unfortunate part is
that we take it out on others who have
little, if anything, to do with the initial
cause of the irritation or agitation.

Random Thoughts from the Cosmos

Life is learning just how far you can push people before they start to resist and start pushing back.

Random Thoughts from the Cosmos

Perhaps it is better to have some moral and ethical values and make some exceptions to the rules (situation morality) than to have no moral or ethical guidelines, but, nonetheless, it should be a matter of personal choice and not because it is against some ordinance or prohibition.

Random Thoughts from the Cosmos

To wage a war in the name of truth is to encounter an unknown enemy who has been conditioned to believe, as you have, that his philosophy of life or religion is more acceptable in the eyes of God than yours. Both sides believe God is on his side, so how can one possibly lose? Even if you are killed defending your ideologies during a war, you have been assured your soul will go directly to heaven or in Scandinavia a place called Valhalla — a place for war-weary Viking warriors.

Random Thoughts from the Cosmos

Let's share with others what we can't use ourselves — some good advice.

Random Thoughts from the Cosmos

At some point or another, we will have to compromise some of our principles and values in order to survive, for you see, most of us are pretty well convinced we could not survive on less than we now have. Oh God! have mercy on a sinner like me. I don't enjoy exaggerating, lying, cheating, deceiving, or making false claims just to maintain my present standard of living. Life really doesn't offer me as many choices as I had deluded myself into believing.

Random Thoughts from the Cosmos

They say that alcohol, tobacco, drugs, and sex are addictions. When people kick a habit so to speak, why is it that they then must find some other substance abuse as a replacement? This obviously proves that they were not addicts, but had a habit which requires some type of oral or physical gratification as a form of sublimation to reduce stress, anxiety, and frustration. The most abused substance for which there is no criminal offense is food. Obesity is a socially acceptable form of behavior. People who have given up cigarettes are often addicted to ice cream, chewing gum, eating constantly between meals, or have to have a "coke" or cup of coffee in their hand whether driving a car, at work, or at home. Obesity causes diabetes, high blood pressure, kidney disease, and strokes. And you want to charge smokers an additional premium for their insurance?

Random Thoughts from the Cosmos

Don't tell me your troubles unless you are seeking advice or a solution. Oh well, why not! Go ahead and tell me. Maybe it will make me feel better if I were to know that there is someone around who has more problems than I have, then that will provide me with an excuse to tell you mine and while my problems are inconsequential and trivial compared to yours, it is always good to get them off my chest.

Comment: Sooner or later, you will discover that if you tell enough people about your problems, you will discover that yours will probably fit into the "norm" category.

Random Thoughts from the Cosmos

If and when the United States is destroyed from within by internal conflicts, what country in the world will be strong enough to intervene and rescue us from our oppressors? Ever since World War II, our primary concern has been that other nations like Russia and China pose a threat to our peace and security for which the U.S.A. has spent billions to protect itself from all foreign intruders — possibly all for naught. When we become so weak from internal strife, that will be the time a major power could conquer this nation with minimum resistance. People will rebel if for no other reason than we have too many laws and ordinances to protect the masses from nobody other than themselves. Freedom of speech, the right to assemble, the right to voice dissent, and the right to protest will be outlawed.

Random Thoughts from the Cosmos

If you have been conditioned to believe that happiness is giving and sharing what you have with others, who could argue with you? It is conceivable that you have a valid point. But most of us have been conditioned to believe that it is more blessed to receive than to give. Take all that you can while the taking is available, as it may be your last chance to accrue a little wealth. Those who give to the church don't always give unselfishly. They hope God will compensate them in some way for their sacrificial giving. Many a minister has said that if you give 10% to the church it will be returned to you tenfold. That's quite an incentive to give if you ask me.

Random Thoughts from the Cosmos

Many wealthy people contend that the public welfare system makes lazy bums out of welfare kids. So what do wealthy families do? They leave their children inheritances of millions which may also make bums out of their children as well. Many will inherit a business or investments which they have had no first hand experience in running or managing. Many heirs will falter and ultimately lose the family fortune. Most people who condemn public welfare support private welfare even though it makes nonproducers out of the inheritors who are seldom challenged or have enough initiative to make a fortune on their own.

Random Thoughts from the Cosmos

If socialism destroys initiative, explain to me why Americans buy Volvo and Saab automobiles and pay 30% more for them than most American cars, which according to popular socialist theories, the quality of workmanship should be inferior because Sweden is a socialist country and the Swedish workers lack the initiative to excel. I think if you compare the standard of living of a Swedish worker with that of an American, you will find the Swedish union auto worker has a higher standard of living than his American counterpart, and thus he has every possible incentive to make a quality automobile.

Random Thoughts from the Cosmos

If socialism is such a deterrent to progress, please explain how a country as small as Sweden can be the second or third largest manufacturer of pharmaceuticals in the world and the leader in the manufacturing of telephones. It only has 8,000,000 people compared to a U.S. population of 256,000,000 or 1/30th of the U.S. head count, and it has a land mass no larger than California. By the way, Denmark has 5,000,000 people and occupies a land mass no larger than Massachusetts and New Hampshire added together, and yet it is probably one if not the oldest republics in the world.

Random Thoughts from the Cosmos

And what's so great about Denmark? It has fewer restrictions on moral behavior than most of the other civilized countries in the world. The Danes just have fun. They have more bicycles than cars and a good rapid transit and ferry system where you can sit and visit with people on their way to work. That is, if they can speak English, which most Scandinavians do. Most are multi-lingual. They are a very small country but big in the manufacture of furniture, electronics, shipbuilding, and beer. After you have had your fill of beer, you can get on the transit and go home without worrying about driving while intoxicated.

Random Thoughts from the Cosmos

Heredity and environment provide us with an excuse to act differently than the rest of society or to blame someone else for the way our lives took a devious turn for the worse at some time or another. There are, however, millions of people in our country who gave life their best shot and are totally committed to being good providers but didn't make anything more than a bare living. It is true there are circumstances which arise from time to time over which we have little or no control which impacts human destiny. The best or worse events in our lives may be yet to come. There are other criteria other than money by which we can judge our fellow man.

Random Thoughts from the Cosmos

Whenever you make a decision based upon past experiences, just remember to take into consideration all the variables which didn't exist previously.

Random Thoughts from the Cosmos

*When people speak of "family values,"
what most are referring to are those
taught by some religious denomination.
Family values, traditionally, were those
taught to children by their parents,
which did not necessarily coincide with
those of any church. Most conservative
churches would like to impose their
values on everyone — even those who
are not Christians. They would like to
enslave the human mind and the wills of
children into nonthinking robots who
will accept the church's code of moral
and behavior on faith alone. Which
denomination, religion, or Bible are we
going to base these values on? To
preserve freedom of choice, it is vital to
keep church and state separate.*

Random Thoughts from the Cosmos

Just what are these "family values" of which the church speaks? Are they referring to smoking, using alcoholic beverages, taking drugs, sexual abstinence, abortion, or pornography? (Gambling has become socially acceptable in this era). Surely we are not speaking about lying, cheating, stealing, or deceiving people. Those who tell you that salvation is for Christians only are deceiving you. Most self-righteous Christians are not so much guilty of sins of the flesh as they are of the spirit. They aren't even aware of the sins they commit on a daily basis. Many fundamentalists are more inclined to accept the values of their ministers than those taught in the Bible.

Random Thoughts from the Cosmos

People trying to make converts are generally trying to convince themselves as well as others that what they preach and teach is truth. They argue that if their teachings sound plausible and are accepted by others, then they must have validity. Otherwise, why would God allow them to teach a false gospel? The Hindus, the Jews, the Buddhists, and the Mormons all have had the same assurances that their doctrines are also infallible. Truth, it seems, is somehow related to their ability to make believers out of those whom they solicit for membership. Why does God tolerate all these games which create nothing but division, enmity, distrust, misunderstanding and wars? God only knows.

Random Thoughts from the Cosmos

Whenever anyone speaks or writes in broad generalities (as the author does), it should challenge you to think about all the exceptions to some of his statements. He shouldn't be offended if you take exception to anything he says. You aren't a good philosopher unless you can see some flaws or cracks in some of your own theories and beliefs. Perhaps there should be a little dialogue between the author and his readers for purposes of clarification.

Random Thoughts from the Cosmos

*Adventure for many is trying to bend
another person's mind into a
configuration that matches his own
beliefs and values. After all we were
created in the image of God, so what's
wrong with fashioning some of our
colleagues' ideas and beliefs after our
own image since we are all an extension
of God? Isn't that what the ministry
and politicians try and do? They make
decisions that have a dramatic effect
upon our lives. They are the elite
members of God's swat team. As to
whose image we were created in, I'm not
sure, but I'm sure that I didn't have
anything to do with it personally.
Collectively, we all are God.*

Random Thoughts from the Cosmos

*The only reform some people are
interested in is tax reform.*

Random Thoughts from the Cosmos

The best way to preserve a marriage is to find some outside interests which each spouse can do individually.

Random Thoughts from the Cosmos

There is nothing that will fragment or cause divisions in our social structure like charter schools and exclusive clubs. We will cease to associate with anyone who doesn't share our beliefs or values. Some day those who have isolated themselves from the rest of society because of those beliefs and values will have to come in contact with reality. Those who have been sheltered from the evils of society by being placed in a private school will be ill-prepared for those waiting to take advantage of these naive souls who have not been alerted to the possibility that the world is full of con-artists, manipulators, frauds, pretenders, embezzlers, swindlers, and insincere people just waiting to exploit their lack of experience.

Random Thoughts from the Cosmos

Don't strip a person of all of his verbal defenses, as he may become violent. You may see flaws in some of his statements but don't press too hard. Always leave him an escape outlet lest you be physically harmed or slandered as humiliation frequently turns to anger or rage.

Random Thoughts from the Cosmos

There are two types of prisons: one is confinement by the use of physical restraints and the other is psychological. Psychological imprisonment is caused by rigid mores, ethics, beliefs, and values, which seal off all the exits to what otherwise might be a creative, adventuresome, and exciting existence.

Random Thoughts from the Cosmos

*Happiness is having a number of beliefs,
prejudices, and opinions which have
never been challenged.*

Random Thoughts from the Cosmos

Small businesses have been on the wane ever since we did away with the graduated income tax schedules. It gave big business more money to expand their buildings and inventories into mammoth operations. The move to adopt an even smaller number of tax brackets would all but eliminate the rest of the small businesses. When we had the graduated tax, even though large retailers could get volume discounts say up to 50%, this could be offset by a 50% difference in income tax rates. In the retail sector small business owners will soon be working for someone else for minimum wages.

Random Thoughts from the Cosmos

Have you ever wanted to be God? You probably are God and don't know it. Everybody knows God so intimately that they think they are His official spokesperson. They become one with the Godhead. So everything goes well in their lives until the irresistible force meets head on with the immovable object. There is always someone challenging God for recognition of his beliefs and theories. Believe me when I say being God isn't nearly as much fun as you might think it is. It's more fun to tend to your garden and watch the flowers and veggies grow while the rest of the world makes fools of themselves playing all their petty and fanatical little "ego" games.

Random Thoughts from the Cosmos

Yes, I recognize the need to believe in something and that's fine (I believe in reincarnation), but don't try to use political processes to make me conform to your unsubstantiated beliefs. If everything that is fun is sinful, don't try to convert me. I'm a hedonist. That's not all bad. For you see, I find pleasure not only in good food, wine, women, song, and a pipe full of tobacco, but I enjoy giving to those less fortunate than myself while being a philanthropist. That's to help balance out whatever else is wrong with me. It's called the laws of compensation and justification.

Random Thoughts from the Cosmos

People who say they have no desire to be competitive are those who can't stand the thought of losing. How are you ever going to get any better if you don't keep score? I know, you are doing it merely as an experiment or for the exercise.

Random Thoughts from the Cosmos

Disappointing as it may be, all my heroes, heroines, and idols evidently have as many problems as I do — if you can believe the tabloids. That is they have all but two — fame and fortune.

Random Thoughts from the Cosmos

Love a philosopher? I think not. After all, they are one of the most despised breeds in the human race. Besides who wants to be associated with a loser. They will try to make you think, and that is something anyone with an ounce of common sense should avoid.

Other people prefer to follow their instincts and habitual patterns of living. Politicians and economists are philosophers of sort. But if anyone is going to change the world, it will probably be an oratorical-type philosopher who has a lot of theories on government, business, morality, religion, economics, and political science who will do it. However, most philosophers have failed time and time again. Even Christ failed but he was more of a law giver than a philosopher. To be sure, Christ was no Aristotle, Plato, or Socrates.

Random Thoughts from the Cosmos

Telling a little white lie is often the margin between success and failure.

Random Thoughts from the Cosmos

The only difference between the American press and Russian press is that in Russia the government tells the press what to print, in the U.S. you can print the truth if you can find out what it is. Unfortunately the press is kind of a moral watchdog which never attacks the credibility of the scriptures as taught by such men as Oral Roberts, Billy Graham, Pat Robertson, and Jerry Falwell; nor does the press question the source of statistics collected by such organizations as the American Cancer Society, the American Medical Association, the Pure Food and Drug Administration, or the EPA. No one ever tries to verify their findings to see if these experts and organizations are ever telling us the truth.

Random Thoughts from the Cosmos

When Franklin D. Roosevelt became president some 50 years ago, the country was in the grips of a depression. How was the problem resolved? We increased federal spending significantly through the Works Project Administration, the National Recovery Act, and the Civilian Conservation Corps programs which put a number of unemployed people back to work. But in order to pay for these additional workers, the wealthy were called upon to pay a significantly higher income tax — as much as 90% for those in the higher brackets, and the economy was beginning to stabilize until World War II came along, which created an even bigger debt because of the cost of manufacturing war weapons and munitions. We had full employment due to a war. But now government employees will lose their jobs in an effort to balance the budget. We are in the crux of a major depression.

Random Thoughts from the Cosmos

A clear conscience may be the result of a poor memory.

Random Thoughts from the Cosmos

Now that we got tobacco smoke pretty well under control, we have a far bigger problem to confront. You probably have figured out by now tobacco smoke is but a small portion of our pollution problem. How about auto emissions and industrial pollutants which infiltrate your lungs causing cancer and other respiratory diseases? But don't expect anything to be done about those since it will take a joint effort by all Americans to clean up our streams and the air we have to breathe 24 hours a day. No one wants to spend billions in tax dollars for a clean environment. They would rather concern themselves over such trivialities as secondary tobacco smoke than tackle a more menacing problem.

Random Thoughts from the Cosmos

One of the questions which has arisen lately is whether cigarettes are more hazardous to your health than people who eat between meals and are obese. When some people give up smoking, they gain an unsightly amount of weight. Smoking is supposedly an addiction, while overeating is supposedly just a bad habit. Is it fair to pick on smokers unless you compare the mortality rates and longevity of life with other types of addictions? People are addicted to caffeine, chocolate, high-fat-high-chloresterol foods, sugar, and ice cream. Where are your longevity statistics on innocent people killed by guns? People are more afraid of being killed by secondary tobacco smoke than guns or alcohol.

Random Thoughts from the Cosmos

Can't you see I suffer from an undernourished ego? In fact, it is about to starve to death. Please tell me how much you appreciate my charm, wit, and intelligence. My ego needs a little reinforcement from time to time.

Random Thoughts from the Cosmos

There is no uniformity in our penal system. Different states have different laws. Different judges have different opinions. Some of the judges are just as hard on first time offenders as they are on seasoned criminals. Most of them are more lenient with people who have money, power, and position than someone of a minority status. There are people serving more time for using drugs than those committing serious crimes. We throw the book at youthful offenders on the theory it will deter other kids from doing likewise. The trouble is the theory doesn't work and you have ruined the life of one who had some potential and a chance to be a good citizen.

Random Thoughts from the Cosmos

What incentive do we offer people to get off welfare? We offer them a minimum wage job which they can't live on from their forty-hour-a-week wages. Many of the poor are paying the same income tax rate as those who make four or five times more than they do. What incentive is there to work if you can't make a living at it? The least we could do is to adjust the minimum wage to the cost of living index. Maybe they can supplement their income by selling drugs or by stealing, robbing, or embezzling. People will do almost anything to feed their families and meet minimal needs.

Random Thoughts from the Cosmos

There is a question I would like to ask a professor of economics and that is: "How does a country like the U.S.A. create new wealth if you don't print money funded by debt?" How can we create wealth when we are importing more goods than we exporting? The day there is no new money supply provided by deficit spending, a goodly number of the wealthy class will then become members of the middle class, and what money is left of the old money will be divided up among those who still remain after the economic reshuffle. To create wealth, it is necessary to process raw materials from domestic sources to create jobs and then to process those raw materials into finished goods. The only thing saving the country's economy up to now is deficit spending for we have no other source for new money.

Random Thoughts from the Cosmos

Should college and university training be available to only those who can afford it? The trouble with the American Educational System compared with the European is some of our brightest children never have the opportunity to go to college while we try to educate others less intelligent merely because they have parental or other financial resources to attend. For this reason we are losing our competitive advantage to other countries who aren't as set in their ways as Americans, who have had it so good for so long, that they have lost their ability to learn from others.

Random Thoughts from the Cosmos

Are there jobs for everyone on welfare? You say, "yes." Well, maybe we can get rid of those people who earn more than minimum wage and replace them with those who are willing to work for minimum wage. Then those who have been replaced will be on welfare. What makes you think everyone is capable of working or can find a job who wants one? Some have physical disabilities. Some have learning disabilities. Others have emotional or psychological disabilities. You see quick food and convenience stores with "Help wanted" signs, but my question is, "Would you work for less than a living wage?"

Random Thoughts from the Cosmos

A vast majority believe that there is a God even though there is little if any tangible evidence to support that claim. But what we know about God comes primarily from the Bible. Most students of the Bible have affirmed that man was created in God's image, thus one can't help but wonder if God wears clothes or does he run around stark naked. If God is naked why should we make all this fuss over nudity? Who then makes His clothes? He surely wears clothes because He wants to conceal his sexuality. Others claim God is pure spirit and can manifest in any form He chooses with or without clothes. Some say they have heard and seen Him, but they lack any tangible evidence or proof.

Random Thoughts from the Cosmos

Most people have little or no interest in politics until shortly before election time at which time they will depend upon bipartisan propaganda as their primary source of information or else they will vote a straight ticket. If people spent as much time reading and studying the issues as they do watching sports and sitcoms on television, they might be able to make some intelligent choices at the polls. Unfortunately, people, in general, have a variety of things they would rather do than debate political issues. Apathy toward politics gives more power to a small minority to seize control of the country when they think the time is right.

Random Thoughts from the Cosmos

If we should ever balance the federal
budget, the banks, and the federally
chartered credit unions along with the
S. & L.s would go under. Why? Because
a bank's solvency is dependent upon
what percentage of its assets are in U.S.
Government Bonds and other types of
securities guaranteed by the government.
If we balance the Budget, all those U.S.
Bonds would cease to exist because of
debt reduction. Now the one thing banks
don't want in the time of a depression
or stock market crash are big portfolios
in real estate and common stocks. The
banks that are most likely to be solvent
are those with the most U.S. Securities
and Bonds.

Random Thoughts from the Cosmos

Politicians are more interested in quick fixes than long term solutions. Besides, whenever something goes amiss, we elect someone from the other party who then has his own ideas as to what is wrong with the country. We are forever going through this process of overturning the political philosophies of those who preceded them. What a waste of time and money. What we need is a multi-party system (more than two) so that no one party has a majority — even a benevolent dictatorship would work better than what we now have. Everytime we come upon a system of governing which works, the other party will convince the electorate it isn't working.

Random Thoughts from the Cosmos

There are many reincarnated Christians living among us today, who still have some lessons to learn before they can progress spiritually. In their previous lives, they evidently failed to learn tolerance, compassion, and to be nonjudgmental of those who did not share all of their beliefs and values. How many more lifetimes will it take them before realizing they have been deceived into believing that entry into one of the higher planes is reserved for Christians only? Some people who have never been churchgoers will progress because of their good works and deeds. Many are humanists, who are atheists and agnostics, who are contributing humanitarian aid to those in dire need.

Random Thoughts from the Cosmos

If you are searching for truth, it does not start or end by studying Christian scriptures. First, ask yourself, "are there any questions which the Bible does not resolve?" It's the unanswered questions for which you should seek answers. That requires some research outside of the Christian framework. There are many books written which deal with all types of spiritual phenomenon and may help you to realize that religion is not a cut-and-dried proposition. There are truths other than those found in the Bible. There is an evolutionary path which you must tread covering many lifetimes before your soul can be liberated from the body.

Random Thoughts from the Cosmos

There are several questions which I have asked ministers over the past twenty years which were never answered to my satisfaction. One was: "Was I predestined to be born into a Christian culture rather than in an Islam, Jewish, Hindu, or Buddhist culture?" It has been reiterated many times from the pulpit that only Christians are saved. "Did I have any choice as to which religion I was to be born in?" The ministerial position generally has been: "We don't have all the answers." Perhaps the answers they don't have, if known, would contradict the ones they affirm to be truth. An astute student of scriptures can find any number of contradictions and paradoxes in the Bible.

Random Thoughts from the Cosmos

Just what is a meaningful relationship between a man and woman anyway?

- *Some say it is merely chemistry or sex.*
- *Some say it is a combined effort to accumulate an estate.*
- *Some say it is having common beliefs and ideals.*
- *Some say it's having common hobbies, recreational activities, and cultural interests.*
- *Some say it is sharing common goals.*
- *Others say it is having and raising a family.*
- *Some say it is caring for and sharing with another.*
- *Some say it is making a commitment and then living by it — come what may.*
- *Some say it is merely an experiment for a short period of time to see if you really have something in common worth sharing.*

Random Thoughts from the Cosmos

If we keep passing laws and ordinances to control human behavior, it will be impossible to sin since all sin will be illegal. How is God going to judge His subjects when they aren't permitted to make choices? Where is this free will the ministry keeps talking about? How can we choose between good and evil when everything evil is going to be outlawed? Some say the only choice we really have is in the acceptance or rejection of Christ. It's hard for some of us who have made a comprehensive study of the Bible to accept it with all its inconsistencies while noting the hypocrisy, arrogance, self-righteousness, and ill-mannered behavior of some Christians.

Random Thoughts from the Cosmos

Many of the nation's kids who were on hard drugs are now on Prozac, Valium, Lithium, Zoloft, Ritalin, etc., which are all mind altering or anti-depressant prescription drugs, may have just as many side-effects as illegal drugs. But how many parents can afford to buy these expensive prescription drugs? Whether they are legal or illegal they are all taken for the same reasons. Drugs are used for depression, anxiety, stress, hyperactivity, etc. Yes, they can even expand your mental output and facilitate learning much the same as "speed cocaine." I don't know of one single university which has ever been allowed to conduct tests on illegal drugs to see if there were any positive and beneficial results. There's no way any university can do any objective research as long as they are illegal. It might prove to be an embarrassment to our federal and local

Random Thoughts from the Cosmos

governments if our universities were permitted to engage in such experimentation and discover drugs did, indeed, have some constructive and positive effects — both physically and psychologically. There is no way our government would ever do a turnabout on illegal drugs no matter how beneficial they might be. The public would be outraged after all this time if illegal drugs were proven to have as many good effects as adverse.

About the Author

My real name is of little or no importance since most of the quotes came from a source outside of myself. I believe that I was destined to write this book, thus I will take no credit for writing it since it was not of my own free will or doing. I felt a divine presence at times influencing my thoughts. Sometimes my thoughts were intertwined with those emanating from the Cosmos. Thus, it has been difficult to separate the two. I am a graduate of the University of Denver receiving a degree in Business Administration. I majored in insurance and minored in accounting. I once owned both an accounting practice and an insurance agency and sold both at the age of 39 and went into semi-retirement. I am now age 70 and currently writing several books — one of which is about my previous lifetime as a country doctor who lived in Calamus, Ia. I am married to a retired school teacher and live in Ft. Collins, Co. I was born in Brush, Colorado — once regarded as a Danish community and have lived in Denmark for brief periods of time. Some of my ideas and thoughts were extracted from the Cosmos and some of my political and social philosophy came from personal contact with the citizenry of Northern Europe.